Knavesmire

York's Great Racecourse
and its Stories

YORK RACES.

Knavesmire
York's Great Racecourse and its Stories
John Stevens

Rowlandson 1802.

PELHAM BOOKS

First published in Great Britain by
Pelham Books Ltd
44 Bedford Square
London WC1B 3DU
1984

British Library Cataloguing in Publication Data

   Stevens, John
     Knavesmire.
     1. Racetracks (Horse-racing) – England – York
     (North Yorkshire)   2. Knavesmire Racecourse –
     History
     I. Title
     798.4′006′842843   SF324

     ISBN 0-7207-1508-3

Printed and bound by Butler & Tanner Ltd, Frome

Contents

Acknowledgements

The author would like to thank the following for their assistance: York Library, York Castle Museum, York Racecourse, The Sisters of the Bar Convent, York, Miss Kathleen Stevens, the late Mr Chris Clarke, Miss Christine Clayton, Mrs Mary Grayston, Mr Norman Railton, York and County Press, Rotherham Library, Sheffield Library, the late Major J. Fairfax-Blakeborough, the villagers of Wentworth and the people of York.

PHOTO CREDITS

The author and publishers are grateful to the following for their help in supplying photographs and for allowing their copyright pictures to be used: Aerofilms page 153; Julian Armytage, dealer in fine sporting prints page 35; BBC Hulton Picture Library pages 93, 121; Castle Museum, York pages 13, 44, 45, 48; Courtauld Institute pages 36, 42, 53, 60, 63, 80, 151; Laurence Cutting pages 181, 182, 183; Mary Evans page 123; Gateshead Technical College page 106; the Earl of Glasgow page 85; the Earl of Halifax pages 47, 51, 150; Provincial Press Agency page 161; Racing Information Bureau page 166; Alec Russell pages 31, 176, 177, 178, 179; Fred Spencer page 180 and items in York Racing Museum; Sport and General pages 10, 11; Mrs C. Thornton 124; Vauxhall Motors page 146; York City Art Gallery pages 15, 29, 32, 38, 55, 62, 64, 67, 68, 70, 71, 77; York Racecourse Committee pages 106, 172, 173; York Racing Museum pages 20, 22, 26, 28, 33, 58, 65, 75, 78, 82, 87, 95, 96, 99, 101, 103, 105, 109, 117, 127, 129, 130, 131, 132, 133, 137, 138, 139, 141, 142, 145, 156, 157, 163, 167, 169; York Reference Library pages 84, 90; *Yorkshire Evening Press* pages 7, 16, 23, 159; *Yorkshire Post* pages 108, 136, 168, 170; the Marquis of Zetland page 106. Every effort has been made to trace copyright owners but in some cases this has not been possible and it is hoped that any such omissions will be excused.

1

Knavesmire's Magnificence... and Misery

 On a glorious day in August 1972 a grey limousine, belonging to York Race Committee chairman Lord Halifax, drew up at the county stand entrance on Knavesmire. From it stepped Queen Elizabeth II. A reigning monarch had come racing at York – the first to do so since Charles I, nearly three hundred and forty years previously.

HM The Queen arrives at York, 16 August 1972.
Left to right: *Major Leslie Petch, John Sanderson, Lord Porchester, the Earl of Halifax.*

From the steep, green bank overlooking the entrance, salvia, alyssum and lobelia roared out a floral greeting in red, white and blue – 'Welcome to York Races'.

Even the mundane racecard had a special cover for that day – a cover of watermarked silk, bearing the Royal coat of arms and the Queen's racing colours of purple and gold.

Knavesmire, home of York Races since 1731, seethed with excitement – a restless carpet of pink faces, panama hats and extravagant dresses. Cloth caps jostled with trilbies as their owners strove to winkle out the best prices from among the never-ending ranks of bookies' stands. A day to be savoured: champagne and lobster; beer and pork pie; tea and cheese sandwiches.

The Queen moved to the County Stand, leaving, to her right, the gentle arcades of the original eighteenth century grandstand. To her left towered the modern 'grand hotel' – the main grandstand which seemed to be keeping a respectful eye on the delicate, whimsical, Regency-styled balustrades of the county stand below.

Through the arrogance and licentiousness of its early middle years, York, potentially the most classical racecourse of all had lost much of its original esteem.

The meeting which, the previous century, had made up almost irretrievable ground by introducing the Great Ebor Handicap and Gimcrack Stakes, was now staging, for the first time, the impressive Benson and Hedges Gold Cup.

For relaxed hysteria there is little to compare with a parade ring. York's was, and is, remarkably vivid, the orange track rendering the central turf impossibly green, particularly when the sun beats down on it, as it was doing on this day of days. Nodding occasionally towards an appreciative audience of two-legged creatures, were three exceptional horses – Brigadier Gerard, Roberto and Rheingold.

Brigadier Gerard, the victor in all his seventeen races, had been voted Horse of the Year. His main protagonists, Roberto and Rheingold, had finished respectively first and second in the Derby. But Roberto, who had experienced a gruelling Derby test, had finished a lowly twelfth out of fourteen in the Irish Sweeps Derby. It was, apparently, a day for basking in the brilliance of the Brigadier. Braulio Baeza, an American jockey who had never ridden in Europe before, partnered Roberto. Joe Mercer was on the Brigadier.

'Jockeys mount'. The tiny procession of man and beast broke away from the seething mass of humanity, across the expanse of Knavesmire, towards the start. At two o'clock to their line, shrouded by the protective, leaf-laden branches of sycamore and chestnut, lay a stone which could tell another story.

'They're under starter's orders'. The best of equine muscle had been cajoled and crammed into the stalls. Behind the horses rolled a lushness which was clipped to an end by the comparative remoteness of the ultimate two-mile marker. The towers of York Minster gazed serenely on.

'They're off'. That little group of wanderers who wished to be there at the beginning recoiled in respect as the stalls exploded and divots spat back from the stalls.

Straight into the bend, with Bishopthorpe Palace, centuries-old home of the Archbishop of York, tucked behind those trees somewhere.

Some straight running, a second bend, then the run for home. But home was some five furlongs away.

Roberto had set a tremendous pace, establishing a lead of some four lengths. Droning over the home straight, like a seasoned bi-plane, was the voice of the commentator. The myriad of human specks round the grandstand was emitting an expectant murmur. Mercer was wondering just when he should ask the ultimate question of the Brigadier. The straight was going on for ever, just as the bend had done.

Three furlongs to go, and now had to be the time. The Brigadier got the message, but Roberto didn't agree with it. At that magical moment everyone, the Queen included, forgot the Queen. She reverted, understandably, to the schoolgirl.

The thirty-five thousand voices funnelled themselves into one throat as Roberto, in record-breaking form, refused to falter in his determination, holding off the gallant Brigadier by three lengths.

A great race. Neither horse had run below his potential. Roberto had simply done better than his best. Such was the impetus of Roberto's finish that his retreating form rapidly merged with the greenery of distant lime trees on Knavesmire Road. While the other horses were being unsaddled Roberto and his jockey were still making their way back - an island, almost lost in a sea of faces.

This meeting put the seal on York's regained eminence. Many, whose opinions were heard with respect, affirmed that the quality of Knavesmire's August racing was the best in the land.

The meeting was to last three days. And the Queen was to grace it throughout. On the second day she would watch Crazy Rhythm break the course record, at the second attempt, in the Johnnie Walker Ebor Handicap. The third day was to feature York's inimitable Gimcrack Stakes, ensuring that a gallant little eighteenth century horse would continue its gallop into immortality.

As Roberto was led in to the winner's enclosure, three of those people who were in at the beginning of the race - a reflective man and his two sons - walked along the opening straight in appreciative contemplation. But the man's brow furrowed as they drew level with the mile-and-three-quarter marker. He glanced up to the trees which were strengthening their ranks around a simple stone, placed on a gloomy pedestal by an incongruous set of steps.

The boys, enraptured by what was so fresh in their memories, reacted to their father's sudden change of mood.

'What's wrong?'

Roberto (Braulio Baeza) is led into the Winner's Enclosure after winning the Benson and Hedges Gold Cup.

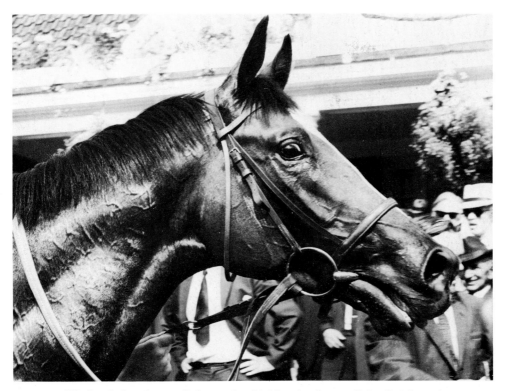

The head of a winner – Roberto after his historic win over Brigadier Gerard.

'Nothing', he replied. 'This is a great day. The best. It's just that I know a lot about Knavesmire. Some of it is a bit grim though. Would you like me to tell you?'

Yes, they would. The afternoon was long and dreamy, so they sat on the warm grass, opened a large bottle of lemonade and unveiled a mound of egg sandwiches. The man began the true story of Knavesmire.

On a hazy August morning in 1800 a horse and cart clattered to a halt outside the women's prison at York Castle. They had come to take Elizabeth to Knavesmire. Elizabeth Johnson had an appointment with another exceptional horse – the 'Three-legged Mare' of Tyburn on which she was to die.

Across the way from the prison stood the Assize Courts, their Renaissance pillars being symmetrically echoed by those of the more recently built prison itself.

At this court, a few days previously, Elizabeth had faced a pomander of sweet-smelling herbs, which prevented the judge from experiencing any stench of her body or rags. She was case number twenty on the calendar of felons, and other malefactors, who were to be paraded before the Honourable

Sir Alan Chambre, Knight, of the Justices of Our Lord the King, and the Honourable Sir Robert Graham, Knight, one of the Barons of our Lord the King.

Elizabeth Johnson was in a total daze as the clerk's voice droned menacingly upwards, surrounding her but unconcerned with her, finding its home in the exquisitely-designed cupola above her head.

'You are charged by the oath of Charles Methley, with feloniously uttering a certain false, forged and counterfeit note, purporting to be a one pound note drawn by the governor and company of the Bank of England; also with uttering two counterfeit half guineas, knowing them to be so false and counterfeit at the time you so uttered them, and with having in your possession other forged and counterfeit notes, half guineas and seven shilling pieces, within the Borough of Pontefract on the 7th day of June instant, with intent to cheat and defraud the said Charles Methley.'

Johnson had passed on forged money. Later records would distort the charge to one of forgery. Why, and where was the true forger?

It was noted at the trial that she was 'totally insensible to what was happening' as sentence of death was passed upon her. Whatever money she possessed must have been so crudely forged as to be easily detected ... by anyone but Elizabeth that is.

Was she shielding someone? Or, more likely, had the money been planted on her?

Elizabeth Johnson had been in that prison since June, and seems to have neither known, nor cared, whether she was guilty or not. To be charged was enough. Anyway, what did 'not guilty' mean? And who was to speak for her?

Now, in August, through the main doors of the women's prison, a tribute to recent methods of incarceration, stepped the sheriff, chaplain and guard.

Making a solemn turn to the left they walked along a corridor of crammed debtors' cells, a corridor of cheerless stone, punctuated by ponderous doors of oak and iron. Oval peepholes were the last connection between the grim world without and the grimmer world within.

Right turn, past the exercise yard to the condemned cell. Never-ending keys and bolts. The final door gave a weary groan as the ever-vigilant warder within eased it back. There was Elizabeth with all the modern amenities at her disposal – iron mesh for her bed, a stone latrine for her relief.

Out with the good book and on with the canting. But Elizabeth couldn't understand a single word that God's representative was uttering.

'On your feet Elizabeth.' Her arms were tightly pinioned and the ceremonial death walk began, back over those stone-flagged floors. Outside one cell an iron flap sprang to attention as some wretch inside pulled on a bell, vainly trying to summon a warder to her plight.

Back to the main doors. A deranged woman screamed her frustration from a cell specially equipped for the mad. A revolving iron trough, set into the forbidding door, enabled her to be fed with her bread and slops in perfect safety.

The female prison, York.

The doors were eased open and the early sun began to light up the flagstones. But Elizabeth didn't notice. There was no audience for Elizabeth – merely the horse, cart and escort. Above her towered the rounded ramparts of Clifford's Tower, setting for a Jewish massacre in the remote days of the Crusades.

She was raised into the cart, where she formed a dazed statue, awaiting a macabre, procession of slightly more than a mile to the dreaded Tyburn.

The hooves clattered their way across the 'Eye' of York – that island of judgment and retribution, studded by courts and cells, all housed behind the finest facades of the day.

The cart approached the high, forbidding wall, which shut in the secrets of the 'Eye', keeping out an ever-alert, morbid rabble. The gateman shuffled to his feet, keys and bolts rattled out a message to the expectant morning as the huge, oak main gates swung back. Castlegate bade her welcome to the exciting life of York.

For Knavesmire was saying farewell not only to Elizabeth, but also to the renowned Sam Chifney, the greatest jockey of his day and a former favourite of the Prince of Wales.

The downfall of Chifney had begun at York, eleven years previously when he was accused of cheating. And he was to suffer the same accusation again.

But he was to die a natural death. For although the sums involved in whatever tricks he might play far exceeded Elizabeth's, they were played within the relative safety of a society which had its own rules, and its own way of dealing with offenders.

Knavesmire was preparing both for Elizabeth and for York Races. August hangings and butchery were good for racing ... and for trade. Hot on the heels of the Assizes, they ensured double entertainment – an irresistible combination for the idly curious or for the depraved. And depravity walked comfortably along these narrow, reeking streets.

Despite the early hour, the streets began to busy as the city of taverns and churches gave its attention to the annual fare of racing and death. Heads turned as the cart rumbled up Castlegate. But eyebrows wrinkled in disappointment as it became apparent that Elizabeth was to be the sole sacrifice of the day.

Where was the usual cortège of misery, where were the hurdles of strapped-in victims whose senses were dimmed by the administrations of innkeepers along the route to death? Merchants and tradesmen were remembering the message of compassion which Wesley had preached in York. Books of prayer guided the conscience of solid enterprise.

Fully aware of their own humble beginnings, the new middle class realised full well that, but for the grace of God, they could have been following the path of Elizabeth Johnson. A new religious awareness frowned on the callous indifference of their times.

Excitement turned to embarrassment. It took the dazed presence of this solitary woman to sum up the sickness of it all. Little meat here for York's professional vultures of the gallows, the ballad-mongers.

Down Nessgate. Many churches, many prayers, but no forgiveness. Over Ouse Bridge and up the steep pull of Micklegate, past houses of Georgian elegance which reflected a wealth due in no small part to the magnetism of horse-racing.

The cart now passed under the medieval towers of Micklegate Bar on the battlements of which had been impaled the head of Richard, Duke of York – 'So that York may look upon the city of York'.

Only fifty-five years before the demise of Elizabeth Johnson these same battlements had borne heads of Culloden prisoners – supporters of the abortive Stuart cause.

The cart dipped towards Knavesmire and evened out for a while, before beginning the two hundred-yard climb to the gallows. There it stood – a grotesque, three-legged framework which could accommodate a score of customers without too much trouble.

Elizabeth Johnson was following a long tradition which she could not appreciate. Here had hung many a man and many a woman – cattle rustlers, petty thieves, petty forgers, highwaymen, idiots, murderers. Some had been innocent, some had been guilty. Some had been tricked, some had been reprieved. But they had all died.

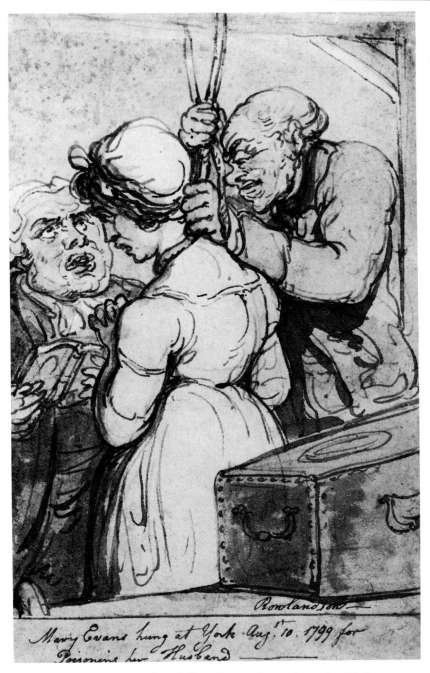

Rowlandson's drawing of Mary Evans who was hanged at York
in August 1799 for poisoning her husband.

The stone on Knavesmire that marks the site of York's Tyburn.

It was here that Dick Turpin perished; here too where 'Swift Nick' Nevison – the gallant highwayman who really did that ride to York – had met his fate.

A crowd surrounded the gallows, a crowd so abject and debased that it could find this a diversion. There were tricksters and pickpockets who were filling in time before racing began. And there were those who simply enjoyed a good hanging.

Behind them lay the huge horseshoe of the racecourse, the centrepiece of which was that delicately-arcaded first grandstand, a tribute to the masterly architect John Carr.

More than ten thousand people could be guaranteed a reasonable view of the dying moments of Knavesmire's condemned. But Elizabeth was hardly a star attraction, and the minds of the vaguely interested were already beginning to wander towards the racing.

The necklace of rope now adorned Elizabeth Johnson, whose glazed eyes saw through the grandstand without realising it. The horse was urged forward and Elizabeth said goodbye both to the little wooden cart and to Knavesmire.

'She was insensible to the last', was the official observation.

As Elizabeth's body ceased its fight to survive word went round that Sir H T Vane's horse, Cockfighter, would not be racing on Knavesmire that day. Vane had accepted a two hundred and fifty guineas forfeit as a horse called Bryan O'Lynn had been pulled out of the challenge. Pity. Never mind, Chifney was here – up from London. And no-one on Knavesmire was disinterested in Chifney. They either admired him or loathed him.

What a bizarre world Knavesmire was in those rakish days: a kaleidoscope of cheats, imposters, eccentrics, heroes and cowards; of debauchery, cock-fighting, outrageous challenges, absurd bets and dignities affronted.

In those long, disreputable days of Knavesmire an alluringly dressed female caused havoc among mankind and hasty hearts among men when she challenged the best of them at horsemanship. The clerk of the course would be sued for withholding prize money from a one-eyed jockey with dirty breeches on the grounds that the rider was no gentleman – a decision which led to an uproarious court hearing, Burdon v Rhodes.

August Assizes, August Races, August hangings. The meeting which was to earn York its ultimate high repute, and which was to ring to the names of Gimcrack and Ebor, wore a different cloak in those days, when four-mile challenge matches thundered across Knavesmire, their followers oblivious to the echoes of the condemned wretches who had screamed their innocence, hours before, on the gallows overlooking the course.

Knavesmire racing grew and, for a time, prospered in the shadow of the Three-legged Mare. It was to attract the society of England, bored with the heaviness of the Hanoverian court in London, and then repel it.

There was inspiration – from the great statesman Lord Rockingham, whose sumptuous assemblies during York Races were the parade ground of fashion; but more specifically from the iron-grey horse Gimcrack, whose gallantry inspired the formation of Ye Ancient Fraternitie of Ye Gimcracks, the oldest racing club in the world.

Gimcrack's gameness, and the ideals he expressed, were to be forgotten for many a year before being recaptured by that Gimcrack Club in the shape of the York Race Committee.

This then was, and is, Knavesmire. How did it all start? The answer to that lies in the distant past when racing began.

2

Early racing in York

 In the year 208 there arrived in Eboracum, later to be known as York, a sixty-two-year-old man whose body was racked by disease. He had travelled northwards through one of the most tenuously held, battle-weary sectors of the far-flung Roman Empire. His name was Lucius Septimus Severus, the most powerful man in the civilised world – a man whose power earned little respect from the sickness which plagued him.

His aim was to suppress the spirit of rebellion in the north of Britain and Eboracum was to be the base of his operations. With him came an army which was probably the largest ever to invade these shores, a display of might which was backed up by a huge contingent of officers and civil officials.

Their arrival had been preceded by a long chain of provisions. This cargo of both the essential and the extravagant sailed up the east coast, bumped and shaken by an unfriendly sea. It found relief in the jaws of the Humber before moving up, on the strong tide, to the Ouse and the haven of Eboracum.

Among the supplies were Arabian racehorses, the first equine aristocrats to set hoof in misty, arthritic Britain. They had been sent to improve morale at this strife-ridden fortress and to give more style and variety to the entertainment there.

Eboracum was lacking the diversions which made the problems of occupation reasonably tolerable. The Ninth Legion, the original Boys of the Old Brigade, had mysteriously disappeared years previously, possibly annihilated.

Their disappearance from Eboracum had left in its wake a half-deserted fortress in the land of the Brigantes, a post vulnerable to the marauding of the Caledonians.

The Romans were back in style, the gardens of the wealthy patricians tumbling from elegant villas down to the banks of the Ouse.

These patricians – civil servants and retired army officers – were the first patrons of racing in York. Anyone of patrician rank wished to emphasise his position, and probably extend his influence, by giving his name and cash to the building of a public monument, to a week of games in the amphitheatre, or to a horse-race meeting.

There was nothing improvised or makeshift about this first racing; it was highly organised, intensely competitive and fully professional. And it appears quite likely that it took place on, or near, the area which was to be known as Knavesmire.

The backer had a manager who hired, or fired, the riders of the team for which he was responsible. The accent was on team racing, with the teams almost invariably being named after colours. So shouts of 'Come on the Greens', or 'Up the Blues', are far from novel.

Betting was heavy, with dicing a popular pastime long before racing came along. The riding was probably hectic and certainly flamboyant, with ribbons streaming from the saddles and harnesses. Nowadays the jockey provides most of the colour.

Severus moved northwards, on a punitive campaign against those who would not let Rome rest. Already a physical wreck, who had to be carried around in a horse litter, he found the exigencies of this expedition too severe, as did many of his troops. The first Roman Emperor to die in Britain, he breathed his last on his return to Eboracum. His body, in full imperial military dress – golden armour with purple tunic and coat – was carried to a funeral pyre just outside the city.

The Romans were to leave Eboracum, but the racing tradition which they had established was to be recaptured centuries later.

We pick up the threads during the reign of Henry VIII, the monarch who sent the leaders of that northern rebellion, the Pilgrimage of Grace, to their gory deaths on Knavesmire less than two hundred years before racing moved to the land of the Tyburn.

In the days of the greatly-feared Henry racing was taking place in the Forest of Galtres, a footpad-infested stretch of greenery which crept up to the medieval walls of York.

The Lord Mayor of York put up a silver bell, to be competed for annually in any convenient open space. Competing must have been purely for the joy of it as the winner had not only to return the bell before the following year's race, but had to compete again for a wager of six shillings and eight pence.

But racing was already trying to spread its wings and the forest was condemned as unsuitable – 'a dreary waste, spreading for twenty miles, where ancient British kings pursued wild boar, wolf and bear'.

There were plenty of open spaces, but the headache was finding one where the horses didn't suddenly disappear up to their knees. York was distinctly soggy, and in those areas which weren't the only feasible activity was punting. For there was a great deal of marsh.

Finding firm going was difficult. And occasional hard going was just that, improvised racing being held on the River Ouse when it froze over in the bitterly-cold winter of 1607–8.

By the time of Charles I frequent racing matches were being held on Acomb Moor, about two miles out of town. And when Charles paid his first visit to York, to see his old friend, Sir Henry Slingsby, he made a point of going racing.

It is Ordered by the FOUNDERS that the Time of Starting appointed by the Articles (viz) between the Hours of Three and Four of the Clock in the Afternoon; be Punctualy Observed; And that if any Rider be not Ready to Start, those that are shall Start without him.

WHEREAS for the Safety of the Riders, the Course has been Corded Round at a great Expence, it is therefore desired, that no Gentlemen or Others will Ride within the Cords.

A List of the Horses to Run at YORK, 1733.

ON Monday the 5th of August, His MAJESTIES 100 Guineas in Specie, to be Run for by Horses &c. Six Years Old, carrying 12 stone, Three Heats.

I. MR. Sheppard's Bay Horse, Dashwood,
II. Mr. Chapman's Bay Horse Nun Mountain,
III. Mr. Clark's Dun Horse, Constant Billy,
IV. Sir Marmaduke Wyvill's Brown Bay Horse,
V. Mr. Hassell's Chesnut Horse, Hum Drum,
VI. Mr. Watton's Brown Horse, Coney Skins,
VII. Mr. Grayson's Grey Mare; Careless, wants a Certificate,
VIII. Duke of Bolton's Black Horse Sifax,
IX. Mr. Thompson's Chesnut Mare, Vixen,
X. Mr. Bartlett's Chesnut Horse, Fear not,
XI. Capt. Appleyard's Chesnut Horse, Quite Cuddy,

ON Tuesday the 7th Thirty Pounds in Specie, by Horses, &c. carrying Eleven stone, Three Heats.

I. MR. Brewster's Bay Mare, Mother Neesom,
II. Mr. Bethell's Brown Horse Partner,
III. Mr. Denton's Grey Mare Modest Moily,

ON Wednesday the 8th. Forty Pounds in Specie, by Horses, &c. Six Years Old, carrying Ten stone, Three Heats.

I. MR. Muster's Brown Bay Horse, Merry Lad,
II. Mr. Clark's Chesnut Horse, Fair Play,
III. Mr. Watton's Brown Horse, Coney Skins,
IV. Mr. Grayham's Bay Gelding,
V. Mr. Thompson's Chesnut Mare, Vixen,
VI. Duke of Bolton's Black Horse, Sifax,
VII. Mr. Hassell's Chesnut Horse, Hum Drum,

ON Thursday the 9th Sixty Pounds in Specie, (called the Ladies Plate) by Horses, &c. Five Years old, carrying Ten stone, One Heat.

I. MR. Fletcher's Brown Horse, Sampson,
II. Mr. Davis's Bay Gelding, Fox,
III. Mr. Bethell's Brown Horse, Poor Robin,
IV. Mr. Bradshaw's Bay Horse, Young Royal,
V. Mr. Brewster's Nutmeg Grey Horse, Audby,
VI. Mr. Waudby's Bay Horse, Jack of the Green,
VII. Lord Lonsdale's Brown Bay Horse,
VIII. Capt. Dilkes's Chesnut Horse, Hob,
IX. Mr. Jessop's Bay Horse, Setbury,
X. Mr. Tunstail's Chesnut Horse, Batchelor,
XI. Sir William Strickland's Brown Bay Horse Surly,
XII. Mr. Hutton's Chesnut Horse, Creeper,

ON Friday the 10th. Twenty Pounds in Specie, will be Run for by Galloways, 14 Hands high, to carry Nine stone, and to allow Weight for Inches, to all under that Height, Three Heats, To be Entered the Day before they Run.

¶ The Ordinary will be on Monday the 6th. of August, at the Black-Swan in Coney-street, and at the George in the same Street, on Tuesday.

YORK: Printed by JOHN JACKSON in Grape-Lane, by Order of the FOUNDERS.

A racecard for a meeting at York, 6 August 1733.

The visit proved a happy one, the King toasting his friend's success as Sir Henry's horse won its race. But the name of York would ring less merrily in his ears eleven years later, for Marston Moor, some eight miles from the city walls, was to turn the tide of fortune against him in the Civil War – a reversal which, ultimately, led to his execution.

Charles I was the last reigning monarch to come racing in York until Elizabeth II in 1972 – the first of many an informal visit to Knavesmire, during which she would witness several personal victories.

But Queen Anne certainly showed great interest in York racing at the beginning of the eighteenth century by providing a gold cup and sending up horses to compete for it. The venue had been switched again, to another swampy stretch – Clifton Ings alongside the Ouse.

Members of the nobility were already being attracted to York. They were settling down to an enjoyable day's racing on the Ings in 1714 when news came of Anne's death. They immediately sought their carriages and made for the city, to hear the proclamation of George I by the Archbishop of York.

The pattern at York was now one race a day during each meeting, with each race divided into heats. The city itself grew keener, and a collection was made for no fewer than five gold plates.

The King's Gold Cup had been competed for in a variety of counties for a number of years. But in 1713 it made its home in York – a matter of considerable prestige. Under its revised name of His Majesty's 100 Guineas, it was to be the opening race at every August meeting for many years.

But in 1730 the Ings proved how unsuitable they were. Yet another new site was needed.

The choice was Knavesmire. A long, undrained bog, on which the poor householders of nearby villages had grazing rights, it had long since earned its gruesome reputation as a place of execution.

It was popularly imagined that Knavesmire gained its name as a mire in which knaves, or criminals, found themselves stuck – a sick joke made sicker by reality.

But a knave was also a menial servant, or extremely poor householder, and the mire was where he could let stray what cattle he possessed.

It was here that Alderman John Telford, a York gardener and seedsman, was given the Herculean task of laying down a racecourse. He was presented with a network of hollows, ant-hills and streams.

The selection of Knavesmire seemed astonishing. But, due either to great foresight or great luck, the choice proved sounder than the ground on which it was based. Telford set to with a vengeance, building arches and laying drains. His course ran round the 'basin', a turn which was subsequently to be regarded by jockeys as extremely awkward and even dangerous. However, a course it was, its roads and layout bearing a link with today's system.

It was first used in 1731, when Telford's beaver-like devotion earned him justified praise. Simon Scrope of Danby-on-Yore, a squire of ancient lineage, wrote ecstatically in his diary:

'Tomorrow we set out for York to see the new horse course, lately made on Knavesmire, and to join in the great goings of the week, the like of which no town or city can compare with for gaiety, sport and company all of one mind.'

Levelled, spread and rolled, this was a new Knavesmire, already ranked as one of the finest courses in the country.

While the course was being prepared three men were hanged on Knavesmire, after their conviction for robbery. Joseph Askwith, Richard Freeman and his brother John, protested their innocence with their dying breaths. For the first time the grim ritual of execution and the breezy world of racing rubbed shoulders.

The opening meeting featured six races, all of which were run over the four miles of the horseshoe. Each race was composed of heats, and each full race occupied an afternoon.

His Majesty's 100 Guineas was the curtain-raiser. Monkey, a bay horse owned by Lord Lonsdale, became the first trophy winner on Knavesmire.

Everything went smoothly through the week, with day two featuring a race for 'aged' horses, day three a plate for six-year-olds, day four a ladies' plate, day five the Galloway Plate and the final day a race for gentlemen riders – a stipulation which, much later in that century, would provide a source of acute embarrassment.

Knavesmire was now to become a focal spot for entertainment, both morbid and lively. Carriages would arrive on the course shortly after miscarriages of justice had been carried out nearby.

With travel to London long, perilous and tedious, and with the Teutonic heaviness of the Hanoverian-style court in London offering little gaiety or inspiration, northern nobility was already looking to York, more specifically to the races, for relief from boredom.

The Lent and August Assizes, with their consequent catalogue of misery, had provided a reasonably adequate diversion. But the new racecourse provided added incentive. The meetings followed the August Assize, probably not by coincidence, and what better than some good racing to follow some good, old-fashioned hangings? Executions could never tax conscience or emotion, as they generally involved people of a distinctly different mould and background.

Cattle grazed on Knavesmire from before 1730 until the 1960s.

The popularity of the August meeting grew year by year – and so did the number of executions. With 'competitive' gallows at other points around the city having long since been removed, Knavesmire became the central execution point of England's largest county, gaining a near monopoly of pre-ordained death.

While horse-riders contested the races, horse thieves went to the gallows. The crime for which Turpin ultimately paid the penalty on Knavesmire was not uncommon in its time. Young William Spink went to the Three-legged Mare only a year after Turpin's appointment.

Meanwhile, back down on the racecourse, events were going their light-hearted way. A poetically-named Jack Come Tickle Me won the fifty pound plate for six-year-olds in 1743. John Singleton, the chestnut colt's jockey, had inspired the title by observing that his mount 'ran all the better after being tickled'.

While Bonnie Prince Charlie was leading an uprising further north, a tiny horse called Ancaster Starling won the plate for aged horses. Never beaten at eleven or twelve stones, this gallant little fellow survived the equally gallant clansmen who were hanged, drawn and quartered on Knavesmire for treason. He died nineteen years later, at the ripe old age of twenty-six.

By the time that great statesman and racing enthusiast Lord Rockingham began his patronage of York races, the variety of entertainment which Knavesmire afforded had become acceptable.

Match 'Em, an outstanding five-year-old, won the Great Subscription Race of 1753 only hours after William Smith had been hanged nearby for murder.

The stallion went on to clear no less than seventeen thousand pounds – at stud – a tremendous sum in those days – and to reach the age of thirty-three.

Smith's body was sent to York County Hospital for dissection, in accordance with a new Act of Parliament. Murders were becoming too rife, and this was viewed as an added deterrent.

When Lord Rockingham's Scampston won the 100 Guineas, Rockingham became the toast of the grandstand. Ironically, Rockingham responded by donating his winnings to the very hospital where Smith's body would be taken apart. Such was the disparity between Rockingham's world and Smith's that this bitter irony would not be appreciated.

While Rockingham was enjoying racing to the full, forty-year-old Edward Wells of Northallerton was contemplating the most satisfying way in which to meet the Knavesmire gallows. Convicted of petty forgery, Wells gave the crowds what they wanted. Casting off his hat, wig and kerchief, and unbuttoning his shirt, he kissed the rope before it was placed round his neck. He then threw himself to his death – 'with great resolution'.

The contrasts became even grimmer. Women who murdered their husbands were convicted of petty treason, causing them to be hanged or strangled before being burned. Mary Ellah met such a fate for strangling her husband through jealousy.

Knavesmire dispensed with many women in this fashion before Queen Charlotte, consort of George III, pleaded for an end to it. Her entreaties were symptomatic of a mood which was ultimately to end the scandal of Knavesmire.

The first execution there was in 1379, soon after Joseph Penny, a York joiner, had been commissioned by the city to build a new gallows. Previous hangings had been carried out near the city walls by the monks of St Mary's Abbey, whose unholy confrontations with the York mobs caused the authorities to revise their death policy.

Edward Hewison, a twenty-year-old soldier, was the first Knavesmire victim. He had raped a girl who was servant at nearby Sheriff Hutton Castle.

By a remarkable co-incidence the last person to be executed there was also a soldier called Edward. Again, rape was the offence. Nineteen-year-old Edward Hughes died in 1801 for raping a village girl. But, by now, such was public sensitivity that a reprieve was sought.

In the meantime the Tyburn cast its shadow over the course. But some glimmer of light was given by Rockingham himself – a glimmer which, much later, would develop into the light of dawn.

3

Lord Rockingham and Gimcrack

 Charles Watson Wentworth was born on May 13, 1730. Number thirteen is commonly considered to be unlucky. But, in this case, it was to prove unlucky neither for England generally, nor, more specifically, for the fortunes of racing in York.

Charles inherited from his father, Sir Thomas Watson Wentworth, soon to become the first Marquess of Rockingham, the lavish estates at Wentworth Woodhouse – rich, undulating land which gazed down on the tiny habitation of Rotherham in South Yorkshire.

Little Charles was to take a great interest in racing, more particularly in the racing at York. Charles I, as we have seen, took a similar interest. But, irony of ironies, that very monarch who revelled in his visit to York, was to sign the death warrant for Thomas Wentworth, Earl of Strafford – the man whose lands were passed down to Charles Watson Wentworth, great patron of racing on Knavesmire and, incidentally, twice Prime Minister of Great Britain.

Charles I had his doubts about placing his signature on Wentworth's death warrant, after Wentworth had been impeached for treason. But the pressures of the mob made him put quill to paper.

Wentworth's head was parted from his body, and the mystery remains as to where the remains were finally laid. In the original, musty, crumbling church at Wentworth village a commemorative plaque to Strafford is repeatedly screwed into the wall. Despite barred doors some force wrenches that plaque from the stonework and flings it to the slabs below. Where is Strafford?

One thing is known: shortly after Strafford went to the block, the monarch who condemned him followed him.

When Charles Watson Wentworth finished his schooling at Westminster his father decided to send him abroad to broaden his outlook. The experiment was an undoubted success. Charles toured France and Italy for about two years, during which time he sailed fairly close to the wind.

While in a coffee house in Bologna he intervened in a quarrel between two Italians, who were preparing for an old fashioned duel. One of them took a deep objection to this foreigner, who was butting into an all-Latin match.

25

Charles Wentworth, Marquess of Rockingham.

He made a full lunge at Wentworth, calling him an English heretic.

Fortunately for both Wentworth and for York races the blade glanced off the button of his coat. The attacker was arrested and taken before the governor, who asked him why he had done such a dastardly deed.

26

'His being a heretic was provocation enough,' replied the desperado.

The governor wished the man to be punished, but Wentworth would have none of it and decided to show this upstart the quality of English heresy. 'If thy religion commands thee to assassinate those who never offended thee, mine obliges me to forgive thee for the attempt.'

It later transpired that jealousy was the motive for the attack. The Italian mistook the future Lord Rockingham for another English nobleman who had taken a fancy to the Italian's wife.

Wentworth became the second marquis at the age of twenty, taking his seat in the House of Lords the following year. His main interest, outside politics, was racing, and he used his power and influence to dominate the racing scene at York.

Rockingham was far from satisfied with the amenities at Knavesmire. Indeed the 'amenities' were conspicuous by their absence. Patron of both the races and the sumptuous evening assemblies, he longed for a building which would cater for the society which the races were attracting.

The Assembly Rooms, with their classical outlines and resplendent chandeliers, formed a more than adequate setting for the card-playing, flaunting, gossiping, flirting and dancing which formed the sequel to a day at the races. But how much longer would these affluent racegoers be forced to witness the sport from the familiar comfort of their carriages?

The answer was provided by a master mason called John Carr who was anxious to spread his wings. He and Rockingham met, forming a lifelong friendship which had its beginnings in the creation of that first grandstand of 1754. Carr rose to the first great challenge of his career – a career which established him as one of the great Georgian architects, and which was to owe its success to racing.

The grandstand was ready for the August meeting. But as a grim prelude to the opening ceremony two men were hanged within clear view of the new building – one for murder and the other for housebreaking.

Luxury at last on the course! Before the grandstand was built carriages had congregated in the centre of the huge horseshoe of an arena, their occupants pivoting perpetually clockwise as they followed the horses round. Now they could watch everything from a verandah. Carr's grandstand emphasised style and entertainment, his main aim being to satisfy the creature comforts. The more practical side of the racing scene – stewardship and administration – would be dealt with later.

A description of the day was charged with admiration, praising the 'convenient offices and rooms for the entertainment of the company. Above these, on the second floor, is a large room for all the company to meet in, which is surrounded by a projecting verandah, with a balustrade before it, supported by a rusticated arcade.'

Meanwhile Rockingham was gaining power by the hour in York. His agent, Jerome Dring, gained the influential position of Clerk of the Peace, causing considerable Corporation resentment; but his hold was really

Carr's grandstand, built in 1754.

strengthened when his friend William Thornton was elected as a Rock-ingham candidate.

The Rockingham Club was formed. Its aim was self-evident – to further his interests in the city. But it had an added purpose – as a recruiting base for the army. The foundations for the Indian Empire were now being laid, and Rockingham gave a guinea to every Yorkshireman who enlisted.

In 1770 another extremely significant club would be formed in York, the Ancient Fraternitie of Ye Gimcracks. Inspired by the grittiness of that little iron-grey horse Gimcrack, it was the first racing club in the world. And it seems more than likely that its roots were bedded in the Rockingham Club.

Nationally, the name of Rockingham was making itself felt, but he was continually falling foul of George III. His strong opposition to George's policies provoked the King into dismissing him as Lord Lieutenant of the North and West Ridings. A staunch Whig, he soon found himself leader of the opposition. In 1765 he became Prime Minister – heading an administra-tion which was to last only a year.

He repealed the Stamp Act, an iniquitous form of taxation which had caused riots in the American colonies. He would have done more, but for the intrigues at court. He resigned in 1766, and was to remain out of office for sixteen years.

During this period of political exile he particularly appreciated his beloved

Knavesmire. And it was here, two years after his political setback, that Rockingham experienced a victory which more than compensated for his disappointment: the renowned Gimcrack was beaten by his own horse, Pilgrim, in the Great Subscription Race. With John Singleton up, Pilgrim was at 2–1, with the great little Gimcrack at evens.

What was so special about this Gimcrack? Why should men group under the banner of its name, dedicate a great race to it and raise their glasses every year to its memory?

Standing slightly more than fourteen hands, Gimcrack galloped through a racing career of eleven years, winning twenty-seven of its thirty-five races. Ironically, although its gameness was the inspiration for the great days of racing at York, it never won on Knavesmire. It passed through many hands – Lord Bolingbroke, Mr Wildman, Count Laranguais, Sir Charles Bunbury and Lord Grosvenor.

While Gimcrack was in France, Count Laranguais backed it, for a heavy

The Assembly Rooms, York, in 1759.

sum, to run twenty-two and a half miles in an hour. This it duly did, before returning to England to continue its winning ways. It was still racing when, in 1770, Ye Ancient Fraternitie of Ye Gimcrack held their first dinner to applaud its pluckiness.

The sight of that gallant little horse galloping into immortality, had to be kept in the mind's eye. More than that, its example was one that all in racing should follow, whatever their role and whatever their responsibility.

Whatever setbacks he suffered politically, Rockingham himself never let Gimcrack out of his mind, and never wavered in his enthusiasm for racing at York.

Under his patronage two hundred and fifty race-shares were taken at twenty-five pounds a share. Each shareholder received a transferable metal ticket, which granted free admission to the grandstand for a hundred years – the period of the lease of the ground by York Corporation. One now appreciates the significance of Dring as Clerk of the Peace.

Carr's grandstand is by no means a thing of the past. Dwarfed by the huge modern grandstand of moving staircases and yawning verandahs, its stone arcade still serves as the champagne and sea food bar – a green-fronted corner of relaxation near the parade ring.

As for Rockingham, he became Prime Minister again, in 1782. During his absence the policy of George III and his advisers had put the nation in a mess. The war with America, which had been dragging on for seven years,

Carr's grandstand today houses the champagne and seafood bar.

was proving cripplingly expensive as well as futile. Widespread waste of public money was alleged, and the undue influence of the crown was causing comparisons to be made between the reign of George and that of Charles I.

Only four months after his appointment, having successfully persuaded the King to seek peace with America, Rockingham died. An old stomach complaint had developed into dropsy.

The Marquess of Rockingham had expressed a wish to be buried without a parade. But the procession to York Minster was something to behold:

> 'There were about two hundred of the citizens on horseback, two and two; twenty carriages with the principal gentlemen of the county and city, who came to attend the funeral of their much loved and lamented friend.
>
> In every street through which the procession passed, the shops were shut and the bells of all the churches tolled.'

Rockingham and Gimcrack, human and equine contemporaries, had set standards. But, as Tyburn continued to demand its toll from the unfortunates up on the hill, racing on the course below forgot all about that plucky little grey horse.

4

Racing with Death

Racing and hangings; gambling and hangings; cock-fighting and hangings; music and hangings – this was race week at York in the eighteenth century.

The Rockinghams of this world were few, and such men could find comfort in an idealism which held little meaning for the pitiful creatures who expired on the hill above the course.

The Marquess would certainly never be seen at an execution. But, just as certainly, he dismissed all thoughts of the Knavesmire anomaly from his mind. To do otherwise would render the pleasures of racing unthinkable.

Even the fleas, which found a living in the turrets of hair sported by the waltzing, giggling, powdered ladies at the post-race assemblies, were in a world of their own. For the fleas of the condemned had far less upon which to feast.

COCKING.

TO be Fought at the ROYAL COCK PIT, BLAKESTREET, YORK, on the 17th of May, and Four following Days:—

		Weight.	
MONDAY, 17th, a Welsh Main for £50	4lb. 0oz.	
TUESDAY, 18th, a Main for £100	4lb. 2oz.	
WEDNESDAY, 19th, a Main for £100	4lb. 4oz.	The highest
THURSDAY, 20th, a Main for £50	4lb. 6oz.	
FRIDAY, 21st, a Main for £50	4lb. 8 to 10oz.	

The Cocks to be taken into the Pens on the 6th of May.

FEEDERS.—Weightman, from Nottinghamshire; Mathers, of York; Baglin. of Newcastle; Reed, of Durham; and Wright, of Pocklington.

The Cocks will be weighed on SATURDAY the 15th; Stags to be allowed One Ounce, and Blenkards Two Ounces.

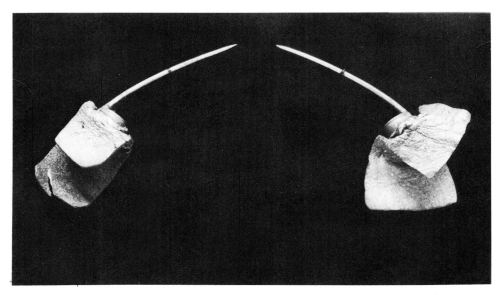

Spurs used in cock-fighting.

The myriad of York inns held awed, hushed audiences as entertainers re-enacted the hangings of the day. Ballad-mongers peddled trashy verses, allegedly the dying words of Tyburn's most recent victims. One doubts that the wretches had given poetry even a passing thought.

Cockpits, reeking of ale and resonating to the yells and curses of the blood-thirsty, were the scene of another sport. For York races drew some of the best 'stags' in the land – birds which hacked at their opponents in blind fury, spurs of silver or steel ripping into feather and flesh until nothing remained but the crow of triumph.

Backers and owners, their hands made sticky by blood-stained coins, sought to vary the odds as the fortune of the battles ebbed and flowed. These were, undoubtedly, some of the best 'mains' of fights in the country.

The final day of the 1756 race meeting at York went into the records as 'a day offering excellent sport'. Entertainment continued the following day, with Elijah Oaks dying 'very penitently' on Knavesmire for burglary. Along-side him were David Evans, condemned for highway robbery and horse-stealing, Richard Varley, another highway robber and John Holsworth, who had broken into a house.

But a contemporary observer at Knavesmire, a fashion expert, who obviously sought his drama in the drawing room, found only the odour of the racetrack offensive:

'The attraction of this, at the best but barbarous diversion, not only draws the country people in vast crowds, but the gentry, nay even the clergy, and prime nobility are mixed among them.

Stars, ribbons and garters here lose their lustre strangely, when the noble peer is dressed like his groom.

To make amends for that, view them at night and their splendour returns; and here it is that York shines indeed. The politeness of the gentlemen, the richness of dress and the remarkable beauty of the ladies cannot be equalled in any part of Europe.'

An alternative to this dazzling colour was the sickening spectacle of hanging, drawing and quartering as four men from Wensleydale, who had caused rioting over the new high prices of corn, were executed for treason. They died 'remarkably penitent, exhorting their countrymen to take warning from their untimely fate.'

Racing, meanwhile, went its merry way, with Knavesmire attracting characters of all shapes and sizes.

Probably the youngest jockey ever to ride in an official race did so on this course. George Stafford Thompson of Thirsk was seven years old and weighed a mere two stones and thirteen pounds when his father lifted him from the family carriage at Knavesmire and placed him on one of his horses to ride in a match.

Mr Thompson had intended to ride himself, mistakenly believing that the condition of the match was 'owners up'. His opponent, however, had hired a Malton featherweight to ride, giving Thompson a weighty problem. He solved it by using a jockey who made the featherweight appear a giant.

Father's instructions to little George were basic: 'Hold your reins tight and, as they say "go" come home as fast as you can'. The boy obliged and won easily, later becoming a fine amateur jockey.

But racing could prove hard for the professionals, many of whom struggled on when their vitality was well past the winning post.

Tom Jackson was sixty years old when he ran his last race on Knavesmire. Striving to go out in style, with an inspired run in His Majesty's 100 Guineas, he finished last, an inevitable consequence of his weak condition.

Jackson, a trainer as well as a jockey, lived only two years after his final race. A tablet in Nunnington village church, his final resting place by the picturesque river Rye, noted that he had been 'worn out in the service of friends'.

The shadow of Knavesmire's darker character continued to lengthen. Ann Richmond – 'a fine young girl', it was sportingly observed – was hanged for setting fire to a stable. Ann Sowerby of Whitby, who had poisoned her husband, was drawn to Knavesmire on a hurdle, then strangled and burned, not long before His Majesty's 100 Guineas opened the racing programme.

During another meeting five men were hanged, some for defacing coins, some for sheep-stealing. On the same day that they paid the penalty a filly called Monimia, offspring of the renowned Match 'Em, won a four-mile

Rosette, ridden by John Shephard, with Carr's grandstand in the background; 1809.

match for the bumper prize of three hundred guineas.

His Majesty's 100 Guineas, over the familiar four miles, was stretched to eight for the first time when Sir G Armitage's Lady Teazle dead-heated with Columbine, Lady Teazle having little trouble in the re-run.

In the Stand Plate of 1776, another of Match 'Em's offspring, the favourite, was coming to the post in the lead but was nearly thrown by a dog crossing the course. The same year saw Eliza Bordington and her lover go to the gallows for poisoning her husband. But, although Eliza Bordington's body was burned close to the gallows, her lover's was left intact.

More prevalent than husband-poisoning was horse-poisoning. The proliferation of betting brought with it many attempts at race-fixing, the crudest methods being employed.

Not long after Eliza Bordington's execution, Miss Nightingale, one of the best mares of her time, raced well on Knavesmire when she took second place in the 400 Guineas sweepstakes. A subsequent meeting, however, found her dead just before she was due to race. When Miss Nightingale was opened up, the cause of her demise was immediately apparent – two pounds of duck-shot, moulded into balls with putty, were in her stomach. A man called William Turner was committed for trial at York Castle, charged with

Stubbs' picture of Dungannon and his constant companion.

poisoning the mare, but was acquitted through lack of evidence.

But, despite the almost desperate decadence of race week, no-one with a genuine interest in the Turf could afford to ignore York. The greatest owners, horses and jockeys went racing at Knavesmire. So renowned were some of the entries that the rest of the field would withdraw. That great stallion Eclipse walked over His Majesty's 100 Guineas in 1770.

So named because he was foaled during the great Eclipse of 1764, Eclipse was never beaten. He won eighteen prizes, including eleven King's Plates, and in seven of them had walk-overs. As a racer and stallion he earned twenty-five thousand pounds, a huge sum in those days.

But even Eclipse couldn't eclipse Euryalus, winner of a plate race on Knavesmire, who had no fewer than eleven walk-overs to his credit. Euryalus gained additional fame by jumping enthusiastically through the window of his box at the Rose and Crown Inn, in the neighbouring town of Beverley, when a brood mare was brought into the yard.

Dungannon, a fine racer, who had a sheep as his constant companion, was well beaten into second place by Phenomenon, in the 100 Guineas Cup of

1784. He and his woolly friend presented a picture of pastoral charm, which was captured on canvas by Stubbs.

Highflyer, winner of a Great Subscription on Knavesmire, was another of the greats. Starting as a five-year-old, he was never beaten and never paid a forfeit. His progeny proved worthy of him, winning a grand total of four hundred and seventy races, and gaining more than one hundred and seventy thousand pounds prize money.

Other horses proved that pedigree wasn't everything. Rubrough managed to win a plate race, even though his dam had been used by a Malton farmer for pulling carts and ploughing.

And while Rubrough was proving his point on the racecourse, a gambler called Ogden was trying to prove another point in the grandstand tavern. Ogden bet some young buck one hundred to one that, if a coin were thrown up seven times he, Ogden, would call 'heads' or 'tails' correctly at least once. He lost.

That wasn't the only near certainty of those days to be beaten. At the August meeting of 1796 Sir Charles Turner's Hambletonian lost the only race of an impressive career when he ran off the course during a three-mile sweepstake.

The same meeting brought ill-fortune to that courageous jockey Benjamin Smith, probably one of the most accident-prone horsemen of all time. Smith was coming to the start on Lord Hamilton's Ironsides in a four-mile subscription race, when another horse kicked out, breaking Smith's leg. Despite the severe handicap, Smith went on to win the race. He was lifted from his mount for the weighing, before being taken by coach to nearby Middlethorpe village for surgery. Born near Huddersfield, Smith died aged fifty-seven years, after a career dogged by repeated accidents. The falls he survived would have put paid to the career of many a man.

Shortly before the Knavesmire meeting in which plucky Smith suffered his accident, three men protested their innocence even as the hangman secured the ropes round their necks. George Fawcett, a man of seventy-seven, was executed for stealing four sheep from a common. The morbid audience was large, but no-one seemed to hear Fawcett's final plea. He had driven the sheep off the common at the request of his two sons; he didn't know he was stealing. The sons had been let off with transportation.

Alongside Fawcett were hanged William Brittain and Thomas Mann, a pair of Bradford wool-combers who, in their dying seconds, disclaimed any part in the house-breaking for which they had been convicted.

If there was any doubt about the injustice of these executions, there was none about that of Michael Simpson.

Simpson, convicted of the murder, by poisoning, of a Thomas Hodgson, was hanged alongside Mary Thorp, sentenced for murdering her illegitimate child. Both bodies were handed over to the surgeons for dissection.

The Knavesmire crowd was unimpressed by Simpson's protests. They had come to watch hangings, not listen to speeches. He hadn't done it?

York City during the Races in 1800 by Rowlandson.

Nonsense. If he hadn't done it, who had? That question was answered eighteen months later when someone else confessed to the murder.

The crowd had paid a little more attention a few years previously when an old man of feeble mind, John Hoyland of Sheffield, told them he would not change places with the men who had sworn his life away. These were the last words of Hoyland, a pathetically harmless man, who had been convicted, on the oaths of labourers John Hunt and William Warburton, of bestiality with an ass.

Hoyland, who had raised a family of near idiots, and who had frequently been thrashed by his own sons, made a distinct impression on those who had turned up to watch him hang. Few doubted his innocence in a case which had much influence on the introduction of a law forbidding the payment of blood money to witnesses. Cash, it was believed, was the sole motive for Hunt and Warburton swearing against him.

In 1792, Elizabeth Elliot, condemned for the murder of another woman, screamed her innocence as the cart of death moved from under her.

James Proctor, an honest man, with a wife and three children, found himself facing the Three-legged Mare after being unjustly convicted of using a forged bill of exchange with intent to defraud. Proctor, who had a grocery and drapery shop in Lancashire, said he was 'sensible to the violation of my country's laws'. The alleged offence involved only fourteen guineas and was easily detected. So he never received a farthing from it. Asked why he offered the money, when he had genuine money on him, Proctor replied that he didn't know the money was forged. This was almost certainly the truth. The case should never have come to court. He made such a good impression that the prosecutor himself, J Beckett, persuaded the judge to sign a petition for clemency.

On the day of execution, April 29, 1786, the hanging was postponed for two hours, in the hope that a reprieve would arrive. It didn't. Proctor's agony was merely extended.

Fate played an even nastier trick, four years later, on a pair of Sheffield button-makers, John Stevens and Thomas Lastley, who were among a group of practical jokers. But the object of the fun, John Warton, was distinctly lacking in humour.

The group of four wanted to drink the evening through. Warton, who was carrying around some mutton, had had enough. So, while his back was turned, the quartet made off with his mutton, finishing up in the inn where Stevens was lodging. They cooked and ate the meat, but clubbed together to remunerate Warton. But Warton, in foul mood, brought a charge of robbery against them. Two were acquitted at York, but Stevens and Lastley were sentenced to death. Warton was held to have sold the pair out, and his house was gutted by an enraged mob.

The Master Cutler of Sheffield, an influential voice in the city, headed a petition for reprieve, which was signed by all the Company of Cutlers and by most of the principal citizens. A horseman galloped off to London to deliver the petition.

Meanwhile, the executions had been fixed for April 17. The two men seemed to have a reasonable chance of survival, but their chief enemy was time. For this was 1790. There were no trains, no telephones, no method of communication, other than by horseback. And the roads from London were filthy, slow and treacherous.

As dawn broke on the day of execution no reprieve had arrived, and the dreaded cart rattled through the gates of York Castle at the appointed time.

Stevens and Lastley, together with four other condemned, were trundled along that everlasting mile to Knavesmire, where a large crowd had gathered round the gallows. The ceremonies began. Time was given for last messages, time during which no breathless messenger, parchment in hand, rushed in to halt the proceedings. The twitching bodies of Stevens and Lastley hung alongside the others. But, at last, the breathless messenger arrived – two days too late. Stevens and Lastley had been reprieved. Everything that the petition had called for had been granted.

The ballad-mongers created some appropriate dying words for Stevens and Lastley:

'We took John Warton's basket and meat,
But not with any intent to keep;
Like Judas he did us betray,
For money he swore our lives away.'

But highwaymen appealed most to the public imagination. Persistently elusive, they appeared to live a carefree life, far removed from the drudgery of their admirers. Frequently, their careers were curtailed by the Knavesmire gallows – among them Amos Lawson, who merrily robbed both Roundhead and Cavalier during the Civil War; the debonair 'Swift Nick' Nevison, a Yorkshireman who gained the admiration of Charles II; and Dick Turpin, alias John Palmer, who was hanged for horse-stealing.

Turpin was to bear the very irons that Nick had borne some fifty years before him. But Turpin inherited not only Swift Nick's fetters, but also a reputation which belonged to the gallant Nevison alone . . .

5

'Stand and deliver'
'Swift-Nick' Nevison and Dick Turpin

 As dawn was breaking, one midsummer day in 1676, William* Nevison, from Pontefract, the same Yorkshire town which had sent the pitiable Elizabeth Johnson to her trial in York, robbed a Kentish traveller at Gad's Hill, four miles from Gravesend. Nevison had planned, and was about to accomplish, the impossible. Leaping onto his bay mare, Nevison sped to Gravesend, where a boat was found to ferry him across the Thames into Essex. William had his connections. He then galloped to Chelmsford, where he paused, probably for about half an hour, to rest his horse.

On he raced to Cambridge – time for another short break. Huntingdon was the next halt – opportunity here for a short nap and a little food. With a little help from his friends, there awaited a fresh horse.

Then, riding at full speed up the Great North Road (and with a little further help from his friends), he reached the outskirts of York before sunset. Nevison had stayed the course, supported by a relay of willing horses and smiling faces.

Entering the city of York, he made straight for an inn where he was known. Making sure that his weary horse was comfortable, he took off his riding cloak and boots, shook off the dust and strolled casually to a nearby bowling green.

In search of an alibi, he had been told that the Lord Mayor of York was playing bowls there. Neither time, nor opportunity, could be lost. He struck up conversation with the Lord Mayor, making a wager with him on the game then in progress. Then, ensuring that both the hour and his presence should make themselves felt, Nevison asked His Lordship the time. Having been informed, Nevison remarked: 'Thus have you taken my bet at a quarter to eight o'clock in the evening.'

The Lord Mayor now had the time, place and person firmly fixed in his mind. Nevison relaxed and, having done so, was quite an affable subject of arrest a few weeks later. Inevitably, Nevison was brought to trial at York,

---

* 'Swift Nick' Nevison is sometimes referred to as William and sometimes as John Nevison. The *Dictionary of National Biography* refers to him as 'John' and it is possible that 'William' was an alias.

charged with the robbery. Inevitably, Nevison called the Lord Mayor to give evidence on his behalf. Inevitably, despite the swearing of witnesses to the contrary, the jury refused to believe that a man could commit a crime in the London area, yet be in York, some two hundred miles away, on the same day.

Ironically, the feat which he accomplished was to be attributed, some fifty years later, to a man of contrasting character.

'Swift Nick' had become a popular figure among the poor of the county, enabling him to operate a protection business. He levied a quarterly toll on northern drovers, in return protecting them from other highwaymen and thieves.

His 'Robin Hood' reputation soon followed. While relaxing in an inn one evening he is said to have overheard a conversation about a poor farmer, with a poor family, who was about to be evicted. The bailiff, who had forced a sale upon the farmer, was among the company. After saying good-night to the landlord, Nevison went up to his room, ostensibly to sleep. He then slipped out of the window, scrambled to the ground and waited, in the shadows, for the bailiff. Out came the villain, and out came his purse. Nevison, it is said, then clambered back through the window into his bedroom, passed a pleasant night and returned the money to the farmer the following day.

Rowlandson's drawing 'Highway Robbery'.

Living by the principle that it is more difficult to hit a moving target, he turned up in the Leicester area to rob three prosperous citizens. He had probably moved out of his area of influence, for the three had him watched. He was arrested and convicted, but, somehow, gained a reprieve. One story has it that the King himself interceded; another that Nevison used bribery.

Then came that remarkable ride to York, after which Nevison was back on the roads with more dash than ever. He revelled in the trick he had played, finding the account of the ride too precious to keep to himself.

Immune from re-arrest, he became the hero of the day, the fame of his exploits spreading to the King. Charles II loved a clever rogue, probably because he was one himself. He observed that Nevison must have ridden 'as swift as Nick', this being the term usually applied to the devil.

The King was so captivated by Nevison's guile that he sent for him and asked him to recount the story of his dash to York. Nevison revelled in the comparison between himself and 'Old Nick', and 'Swift Nick' he was to be for the remaining eight years of his colourful career: a truly apt nick-name.

Nevison who had once served with the Duke of York in Flanders, must have felt that he was living a charmed life. If the King admired him, then the fates must be with him too. Although, in theory, divine right had disappeared with the death of the King's father on the block, the aura of it must have surrounded Charles II.

Nevison was now concentrating on the highway between Newark and York. His robberies were frequent and daring – so daring in fact that he was caught again and jailed in York. Once more he escaped, leaving behind an infuriated Sir John Reresby, governor of York Castle.

'Swift Nick' had made a fool out of many in York, and Sir John did not revel in being top of the list. On October 23 1681, the indignant governor saw the King and told him of Nevison's escape. The scoundrel, said Sir John, had committed several notorious robberies, and it was with 'great endeavour and trouble that I had got him apprehended in the first place'.

Charles probably found Reresby tedious. Nevison was of definite entertainment value. So, when Sir John asked the King to issue a proclamation against Nevison, Charles refused, pointing out that such notice would cost him one hundred pounds.

The King, however, had to go through the motions of indignation. He ordered a twenty pound reward for Nevison's capture. Sir John recorded that Nevison was caught 'not long after'. But this was nonsense; Nevison still had three good years left in him.

The reward money was by no means enough to persuade the public and innkeepers of Yorkshire to hand Nevison over. The King probably realised this when he fixed the amount. Nevison was able to walk the streets of his favourite resting place, Wakefield, unmolested and to enjoy his drinking in peace.

Eventually, however, the reward did prove tempting – to a butcher named Fletcher, who headed a group which attempted to take Nevison. Swift Nick drew his pistols and shot Fletcher, his only known act of violence in more than thirty years of crime.

His fate was now closing in on him, and it seems apt that his career should draw to a close at about the same time as that of his admirer, the King.

The hunt was on for Nevison. Even an escapologist of his calibre needed to rest sometimes, and Nevison was literally caught napping, Captain William Hardcastle finding him snoozing at the Three Houses Inn near Wakefield.

There was no escape this time. He was put into leg-irons at York Castle Prison. These same irons, weighing more than twenty-eight pounds, were to be worn by Dick Turpin, the man who was also to inherit Nevison's reputation.

Nevison was led through York's streets to Knavesmire on May 4 1684. His prayers said, Swift Nick mounted the ladder to his death. No false bravado, no brash gestures.

Though he and Turpin shared the same fetters, this was all they had in common. Nevison – tall, gentlemanly, courageous and of pleasing appearance – was the Claude Duval of the north, expressing all those qualities which a romantically-inclined public was later to expect from a highwayman.

Turpin, who made a fine show of his final hours, before being executed on Knavesmire, had been cruel and uncouth. His conviction at York was for

Leg irons, now in the Castle Museum York, which were worn by both Nevison and Turpin.

Lord Rockingham and Alabuclia with Wentworth Woodhouse in the background, painted by Killingbeck. (Sothebys)

The legendary Gimcrack painted by Stubbs. (From the Earl of Halifax's collection)

Entertainments at York Races 1769. (York City Art Gallery)

Rowlandson's cartoon of York Races. (York Racing Museum)

Dick Turpin from a contemporary print.

horse-stealing, but his arrest was caused by his shooting a cockerel, after a poor day's sport in East Yorkshire had prompted one of his filthy moods.

His main claim to fame is the way in which he faced death on Knavesmire – with an apparent contempt which drew gasps of admiration from the crowds. The debased public of those days, deprived of an adequate life, drew some inspiration from a man who died well. Possibly the other side was preferable to the one of which they had experienced.

A great death, however, must have been preceded by a great life. In this way, probably, did the demise of Turpin saddle the back of Nevison's exploits. The tail of the story was given a horse, thanks to the ballad-mongers. Nevison's horses became the Black Bess of horse-stealer Turpin.

Son of an Essex farmer, Turpin's career was studded with acts of brutality. A description of him, issued in a proclamation, forms a marked contrast to that of his predecessor Nevison: 'About five feet nine inches high, very much marked with the small-pox, his cheek bones broad, his visage short'. Turpin's natural endowments appear to have been a direct reflection of his personality.

A butcher by trade, he married a woman called Palmer, took to cattle-stealing, to smuggling and then to deer-stealing in Epping Forest. He and his gang then turned to house-breaking, often behaving abominably. They are said to have thrown scalding water over one householder. On another occasion a maid-servant is said to have been raped.

Turpin then went into business with a highwayman called King, operating from a roadside cave in Epping Forest. He killed the servant of a forest-keeper who tried to arrest him, and later shot King, possibly by accident.

Life in the south was now too precarious, so Turpin moved up to Lincolnshire, where horse-thieving, the offence which led to his ultimate indictment, became his trade.

After escaping from a constable, who had arrested him, Turpin moved to Yorkshire, using his wife's name of Palmer and posing as a gentleman. He often accompanied men of good name on hunting and shooting expeditions, and it was at this time that his quick temper got the better of him. A poor day's outing caused him to shoot a cockerel belonging to his landlord. When a certain Mr Hall rebuked him for his bad form, Turpin told him that he too would be shot if he were to hang around much longer.

A warrant was issued, and Turpin was brought before the justices at Beverley. Had the complaints ended here Turpin would probably have gone sailing on. But someone accused him of horse-stealing – a capital offence. Turpin had to go for trial in York.

He appeared on the indictment as Palmer, and it was as Palmer that he was convicted. But the revelation of his true identity was made when his former schoolmaster identified his hand-writing in a letter which Turpin had sent from jail. Turpin, a much-wanted man, became an incarcerated attraction, people coming to York from far and wide in an attempt to clap eyes on him.

Dick Turpin was determined to go out like a lion, not a lamb. In so far as a condemned man could revel in his last days, he did so.

Through bribing the turnkeys, friends of the condemned were able to pass on pathetic presents of white caps, black ribbons, nosegays and oranges, so that the doomed could make an 'attractive' journey to Knavesmire. Turpin chose his own going-out dress – a new fustian frock and a pair of pumps.

On the eve of his execution, the final macabre touch was added, Turpin hiring five poor men, at ten shillings each, to follow the cart to Tyburn as mourners. He distributed hat-bands and gloves among others, and left a ring and other articles to a married woman in Lincolnshire, with whom he had been acquainted.

The legend of Dick Turpin began with his end – with the inevitable rickety ride to Knavesmire. Along the entire route, followed by his hired mourners, Turpin bowed to the thousands of spectators, with an astonishing air of indifference.

He mounted the ladder to the rope with apparent firmness and determination. When his right leg began to tremble he stamped it down, with the annoyance of a man ashamed that this might denote a trace of fear. A steady buzz of admiration arose from the crowd as Turpin chatted to the hangman. Then, suddenly, the rope around his neck, he threw himself from the ladder to his death.

After a few minutes he was pronounced dead. A hush had descended upon a rabble which was deeply affected by Turpin's apparent contempt for death.

This letter was written by Turpin to the owner of a barn at Cantley, near Doncaster, where Turpin took refuge. The letter reads:

I, William Turpin, highwayman, was drove here by stress of weather and fear of being discovered, but I desire you, dear friend, you who belongs this barn, not to make any discovery of anybody being here, for I am forced to stay in this neighbourhood for a considerable time, and shall not do much more mischief than I have done you this night, to anybody hereabouts. You have perhaps heard that there is a great reward offered for taking me, but let not that make you endeavour to seek my ruin, who means you no harm. Perhaps I may be forced to lye another night.

Deranged prisoners in York Prison were given their food in this feeding trough.

Hired hands or not, Turpin's mourners were determined to stand by him, even after death. Keeping the crowd at bay, they carried his body to the Blue Boar Inn in Castlegate, retracing much of the route that Turpin had made to his death. The landlord had almost certainly plied Turpin with drink during that sickening death ride.

The body was left in the Blue Boar overnight, before being taken to St George's graveyard for burial the following morning. A rough inscription on the coffin bore Turpin's initials and age.

Turpin must have made a tremendous impression on those hired mourners. Any financial considerations had ceased at the gallows, but here they still were, digging his grave as deep as possible, to protect the body from trophy-mongers, body-snatchers and dissectors.

But, by the following morning, it had disappeared.

There began, throughout the city, a bizarre hunt for the body of Dick Turpin. A group of local people toured the most likely places. Sure enough, they found the corpse in a surgeon's garden, where it had been taken by body-snatchers.

The crowd, still accompanied no doubt by those faithful mourners, laid the body on a board and carried it, through the streets, back to the graveyard. The corpse was placed back in the coffin, which was then topped up with lime and re-buried in the original grave.

Today the heavily-reinforced grave bears a plain, hefty headstone, dominating a modest graveyard.

Shortly after Turpin's remains had found permanent rest, Sedbury, a highly-esteemed racehorse, won his race near the very spot where Turpin had been hanged.

There were thirty-six carriages on the course when Sedbury, 'a horse of great beauty and exquisite symmetry', triumphed in the ladies' plate.

Andrew Wilkinson, of nearby Boroughbridge, who sold the chestnut for a mere five guineas, was to rue the parting with the best horse of its day. Sedbury died in 1759, at the age of twenty-five.

Invariably, racing at York in the eighteenth century bore the stamp of the barbarity and decadence which surrounded it. Although society had been attracted to Knavesmire, the mood of self-indulgence became easily translated into decadence and, without a purposeful hand at the helm, the ship was set on an aimless course of floundering which would continue into the following century.

Where was the book of rules? Unwritten. Where was the code of conduct? Forgotten. Who was to give advice? Anyone.

Events, of course, were not without their lighter side and, in 1791, before even a ray of enlightenment had pierced through the Knavesmire clouds, a race was held which epitomised the degeneration of York races.

6

What is a Gentleman?
The uproarious case of Burdon v Rhodes

 The race which was to provide the main topic of conversation for months to come was a spring-meeting sweepstakes for hunters – for true, practising hunters, which had never won 'plate, match or sweepstake'. Little did the participants realise that they were creating a piece of pure comedy.

Each horse had to carry twelve stones weight, belong to a subscriber to the stakes and to be ridden by a gentleman. It was the last condition, until then unchallenged in racing circles, which caused the controversy.

It was easy to present credentials for the horse: a hunter was usually certified as being a runner with a particular hunt. The lack of any track record could also be confirmed. Checking the weights was basic racing procedure. But who carried a certificate to prove the rank of gentleman?

In those days it was tacitly assumed that the title of gentleman was a right of birth, and could not be earned or bought – an outlook which persists in some circles even today. Good manners were no qualification. If a gentleman had them all well and good. But he could get along very nicely without them. If a man did not earn a living, and had no particular desire to do so, then he had little alternative but to be a gentleman.

The trouble started at the weighing-in, when 'honourable' horsemen of the day were joined by a weird-looking character, whose age, it later transpired was well into the seventies. His name was Kitty Rowntree, a small-holder who was frequently seen in the company of farmers, enjoying plain food in common eating-houses. He was one-eyed, and wore dirty leather breeches and an old wig, to be described later by a witness as 'not worth eightpence'.

Rowntree had been hired by Mr Thomas Burdon to ride a horse called Centaur. Rowntree himself wasn't too happy about accepting the ride, as he had a fair idea of the type of company against whom he would be competing. In addition, it appeared, Burdon was slightly the worse for drink when he hired Rowntree. But Rowntree promised to ride in the race, despite the inevitable embarrassment.

The gentlemen horsemen conspired to snub Rowntree from the moment he weighed in. They made no secret of this at the subsequent court hearing. In fact they were rather proud of it. They had seen Rowntree compete with

Turfites – Knavesmire's seasoned regulars of the eighteenth century – by Rowlandson.

others of his ilk and, until then, had no reason to take exception to him as a person. But his entering that race could be viewed only as the height of impertinence.

One or two of the riders sidled up to Rowntree and quietly hinted that it might be a good idea if he withdrew. Rowntree, equally quietly, refused. The gentlemen then held an unofficial meeting. One or two complained to the Clerk of the Course, Mr Robert Rhodes, who, regretfully at that stage, could do nothing. There was only one way to bring home to Rowntree, and to others who might emulate him, the gravity of the situation. He must be treated as an outsider, literally, during the race itself.

This meant that the 'gentlemen' would adopt double values. They would join the race, but would not compete against Rowntree. Centaur would run on his own, with the others jollying along a smug distance away.

Not surprisingly, Centaur, with Rowntree up, won the race.

Now the fat was really in the fire! The exclusive bunch, busily having a race of their own, were furious.

Second past the post, the leader of that other world, was a Mr Chichester, who stormed up to Rhodes, insisting that he, Chichester, was the true winner. Rhodes, who was probably acutely embarrassed, had to show favour. These men, despite their pretentiousness, had real power. Rowntree had nothing but his smallholding and his old wig.

The sweepstakes had been deposited with Rhodes, as Clerk of the Course, and it was his duty to pay out. But Chichester insisted on objecting that Rowntree was no gentleman, that he failed to meet the conditions of the race and that the win was void.

Rhodes, it appears, wavered, but Chichester promised to indemnify him against any action taken against him. So Rhodes refused to part with the money.

This was a slap in the face not simply for Rowntree, who by now must have been sick of the whole affair, but for Centaur's owner, Thomas Burdon, who seems to have been on the periphery of society and very keen to stake his place. Burdon, rightly, regarded the decision as an insult, and decided to take action against Rhodes, who was to act as a mere front man for Chichester. But Rhodes was the nominal defendant, and the two discussed the best way for settling the dispute.

The Jockey Club was suggested as the suitable arbitrator. But Burdon insisted that a point of honour was at stake. He chose to go to law.

The case was put down for hearing before Mr Baron Thomson and a special jury at York Guildhall the following August. It was heard early in the month, avoiding a clash with the August meeting.

During the months between the race and the hearing York was abuzz with speculation. Was Rowntree a gentleman or not? So many people could identify with Rowntree. If he made it, so could they.

The trial was fixed for seven o'clock in the evening. Streets adjoining the Guildhall were packed with people hours before the start. The crowds upset the judge so much that he turned up an hour late. When he did arrive he found that the boxes reserved for jurors and witnesses were brimming over with people who had no right to be in them. Swearing in the jury was a major task because of the noise.

After repeated warnings from an exasperated judge, the hearing got underway. The claim, by Mr Burdon, was for the one hundred and twenty-three pounds sweepstakes which had been withheld from him. If he won his claim it would automatically follow that Rowntree could be regarded as a gentleman and that he, Burdon, had acted quite properly in engaging Rowntree in the first place.

An 'ordinary' eating house. Rowntree's status was questioned as he was known to frequent such a place.

Mr Law, senior counsel for the plaintiff, Burdon, outlined the claim before calling his first witness, Sir William Foulis, who seemed to be the right sort of person to open the innings. Sir William confirmed that Mr Burdon's horses, Centaur and Ticket, hunted with his hounds, and produced their hunting certificates. Yes, he knew Rowntree, as he lived in his neighbourhood. Rowntree sometimes joined the hunt.

'Do you regard him as a gentleman?', asked Mr Law.

'Not in the general acceptation of the word', was the disappointing reply.

'Does he enjoy the sports of the field and kill game like any other gentleman?' asked Mr Law, scrambling to regain lost ground.

'I suppose so, he takes out a licence,' said Sir William, still unimpressed.

According to Sir William, Rowntree had been hunting before he, Sir William, was born. The witness was singularly lacking in enthusiasm.

Mr Law threw a last, despairing question: 'Did you ever know him do a dirty action?'

'I never did,' vowed Sir William.

Next to the stand was a John Preston, farmer, a good friend of Rowntree. Did he reckon Kitty Rowntree to be a gentleman?

'Aye, to be sure I do', replied the faithful John. Kitty, he said, went to the markets like other farmers.

Honest John felt the full brunt of county prejudice when defence counsel cross-examined. Rowntree did indeed dine with other farmers in a common eating house, termed 'an ordinary' in those days. The place, it transpired, was so basic that the expenses involved seldom exceeded one shilling per head.

Mr James Rule, who witnessed the weighing-in, didn't do the plaintiff's case much good either, referring to Rowntree as 'an old gentleman with one eye, dirty leather breeches and an old wig not worth eightpence'. Did he consider Rowntree a gentleman?

'He may be one, but he has not much that appearance', replied the obnoxious Mr Rule.

The senior counsel for the defence, Mr Chambre, addressed the jury before calling his own witnesses.

The subscribers, he admitted, were free to choose their own riders. 'But could it be that such a man as Rowntree would be permitted to ride? That a man, like as he has been represented to you, was a fit person to keep company with, even in a ride, the other gentlemen who ride. Good God! Gentlemen (note the choice of address by counsel) can you for a moment believe it was the intention of the parties that a man of his description should ride?'

This clumsy, tactless address must have helped damn the defence case. Our Mr Chambre was obviously in such a world of his own that he failed to appreciate the social position of most of the jurors.

In informing the jurors that men like Rowntree were unfit to ride with gentlemen he automatically categorised as unworthy the jurors themselves. Probably small traders, they would more readily identify with Rowntree than with those who claimed to be his social peers.

Moreover, having been so presumptuous, counsel then went on to court the jurors' favour by addressing them as gentlemen, the very title which, in statement, he had denied them. Mr Chambre, now obviously feeling slightly guilty about his brief, softened his approach:

'We mean not to depreciate the character of Mr Rowntree (you could, after all, be a gentleman and have little character) to arraign any part of his conduct, even on this occasion, for he seems to have been made the unwilling instrument of another's want of propriety.'

Now the attack was on Mr Burdon who, allegedly, should have had more sense of occasion than to enter so incongruous an object as Rowntree as a rider in this race.

Mr Chambre then resumed his illogical way: 'We oppose not his (Rowntree's) pretentions to merit. He may possess as much as those in a superior station of life. It is only to the character of a gentleman that we mean to resist his claims.'

Then, having exhausted every paradox at his disposal, Mr Chambre proceeded to call his witnesses.

A steward at the meeting, Mr Robert Denison, told how Chichester objected to Rowntree riding in the race.

George Baker, one of the subscribers to the sweepstakes, and a well

Execution day at York, as the procession makes its way through Mickelgate Bar. The Tudor architecture on the right is formed from Rowlandson's imagination.

entrenched gentleman into the bargain, said that Burdon himself was beyond the pale, never mind Rowntree.

Mr Baker reveals an obnoxious arrogance, which must have been prevalent in his circle, as he describes his objections to both men:

'I have objected to similar people, and they have generally submitted to my objections, particularly to Mr Burdon himself, to whose riding, as a gentleman, I have objected both at York and Preston races. At the latter place Mr Burdon submitted to my objections and did not ride.' (Was this why Burdon used Rowntree to ride his horse at York?)

Baker said he asked Rowntree 'how he could make such a fool of himself in his old age, as to ride for a gentleman'.

'What answer did he make?', asked Mr Chambre.

'He said he was sorry he came, that he did not pretend to be a gentleman, that he had made a promise to Burdon, when he was drunk, to ride his horse for him, and that he would sooner go home dead than break his word.'

Mr Law seized his opportunity with relish. 'Surely,' he murmured loudly, 'this is a little symptomatic of a gentleman. He seems to be the very pink of gentility.'

The Hon. George Monson, a rider in the race, said he told the Clerk of the Course (Rhodes) that he would not ride with Rowntree.

Mr Chambre said, 'Mr Rowntree, however, rode. Did you ride against him?'

'I took no notice of him at all, but rode with the other gentlemen,' replied Monson.

John Warton, a neighbour of Rowntree, and a Jockey Club member, was asked if Rowntree kept hounds. To keep hounds was gentlemanly. To have dogs wandering around was not.

'He has a few couples', condescended Mr Warton, 'which live upon the tenants. Six or seven perhaps'.

Mr Chambre asked, 'In the common sense of the term "keeping hounds" do you regard Mr Rowntree as doing so?'

'Certainly not!' was Mr Warton's reply.

Did he consider Rowntree a gentleman?

'Neither Mr Burdon nor Mr Rowntree is, in my opinion, a gentleman.'

Mr Law sprang to his feet, objecting to the affront to his client, Mr Burdon, whom he considered to be under his immediate protection.

The affronts, the sneers, became even worse. Another subscriber to the sweepstakes, Mr Christopher Wilson, proved he could be as obnoxious as the worst:

'I saw Rowntree on the race-ground. He certainly is not such a man as we intended should ride. He would be objected to on any race-ground in England. I have rode in similar sweepstakes for several, for the Prince of Wales (George's name seemed to be dragged into any controversial racing issue of the time) and I am certain if Rowntree had attempted to ride on such occasions he would have been kicked off the course.'

To round off the defence case the final witness claimed that Rowntree kept hounds 'no more than I do a pack of archbishops'.

The defence had been crude and arrogant, and Mr Law, sensing the court's feeling for the underdog, took full advantage of the summing up. His speech was masterly and convincing, taking full advantage of the powerful prejudice against the defenceless Rowntree.

No-one, said Mr Law, had defined a gentleman. They had criticised Rowntree's dress and eating habits, but what criteria were these?

'Sarcasms have been thrown out against him for going to market and dining at an ordinary at one shilling and one shilling and sixpence per head. I think there are many of much greater consequence and importance in the scale of society, both as to fortune and rank, than most who now hear me, and about whose pretentions to the title of gentleman there could be no dispute, who have dined at much less sum, and perhaps in much less respectable company, than that of honest reputable farmers.'

Rowntree had a small estate, enjoyed the sports of the field, took out a licence to kill game and helped other gentlemen in preserving it from poachers.

'He follows no other occupation or business but pleasure, and if to be idle and useless is one of the prominent features of a gentleman, he has most fully in this instance proved his claim to that distinction. But when to these requisites I add the nicest sense of honour, the strictest adherence to a promise, that exquisite sensibility which is prepared to meet public insult, as well as private inconvenience, rather than break a promise made in a moment of partial inebriety, I think his character, on such a view of it, must stand high in the estimation of every man of honour.'

The Guildhall resounded with applause, particularly in the body of the hall. So great was the noise that the judge rose to his feet, turned to the Lord Mayor, who was sitting alongside him, and asked him to call for constables 'to preserve the peace of the court'.

Cheers and applause still filling the hall, the Lord Mayor went out to order more candles, so that the offenders could be seen, as well as heard.

Mr Law, now in full flight, went on to attack the distortion that had been made of Rowntree's virtues. 'Shall an honest, respectable character, in whom every public and private virtue is united ... be degraded as the scum of the earth, for daring to claim to that rank in life which his conduct and situation entitle him to?'

At this point Mr Law was subjected to heckling by a group of undisputed gentlemen in the court. Mr Law continued through the heckling, which he now took personally. 'The insult I have received cannot fail to make a lasting impression upon me,' he said, before making the most telling indictment of all.

Every self-styled gentleman took great pride in his sportsmanship, in his being a good loser and a magnanimous winner. Relatively few really possessed this quality, but to infer so was to tread on the most delicate of grounds. It was the stuff that horse-whippings were made of.

Revelling in the privilege afforded by the court, Mr Law delivered the coup-de-grace.

'Can it be doubted that the term gentleman is here opposed to jockey or groom, that the intention of the subscribers was that none of the horses should be rode by men whose professional skill would give them an evident advantage over their competitors, and over-match the others in point of jockeyship?'

The court broke up, and the judge went to his lodgings, asking the jury to bring their verdict with them.

The jury's deliberation was short, and a huge crowd followed them to the lodgings, where the judge was informed that they had found for the plaintiff, Mr Burdon.

So ended a unique hearing, called to test one of the most vexing social questions of all, a question which will always be unanswerable – what is a gentleman?

Ironically, Rowntree, the man without apparent claim to the title, came nearest to fulfilling the requirements. He was a gentleman, chiefly because he did not acknowledge himself so to be.

Badges for subscribers to the new stand.

The man with the dirty breeches and old wig had shamed his so-called betters, and Knavesmire had brought to the head an issue which had begun to fester throughout the sporting world, and which would continue to do so for a long time to come.

A modest man's reputation had been enhanced. But, at about the same time, Knavesmire would see tarnished the reputation of a famous, successful man.

7

Sam Chifney
The fall from grace of a royal jockey

 In the very month that the humble, ageing smallholder Kitty Rowntree was elevated to the rank of gentleman, the most famous jockey of his day, Sam Chifney, was accused of cheating at Knavesmire.

The fall from grace of the royal jockey, pride of the Prince of Wales, began at York. Already envied by northern jockeys for his flair and popular success, the Newmarket-trained Chifney was one of the first professionals to find that life can be tough at the top. Traveller was the horse which made, then broke him, at York. Traveller would travel with him throughout the rest of his career.

Only two years previously, in 1789, he and Traveller came to York as an unbeatable combination. Chifney, noted for his loose-rein riding, boasted that he could beat any northerner put against him.

The Prince of Wales and the Duke of York were present at Knavesmire to see Chifney, on Traveller, take on the best the north could muster in a four-mile subscription purse.

If, and only if, Traveller won this race, he was to be sold to his Royal Highness for one thousand, five hundred guineas, a hefty sum in those days.

Chifney was the hero of the day when he won conclusively. The meeting had drawn a huge influx of nobility and gentry from throughout the land, and the win made George feel that he was already a king.

Flushed with success, the Prince went to York's Theatre Royal in the evening, before continuing his celebrations into the following morning at the traditional race-week dance in the Assembly Rooms. York race-week was still a highlight of the social year, when the impoverished would gather in the mud outside to witness the height of fashion sweep into the Assembly Rooms for the dances, concerts and card parties.

Chifney was riding high, but his favour with the Prince was to be relatively short-lived. George was to disown Chifney, and to give up most of his connections with racing. Lacking that royal touch, the true decadence of York races was to be underlined.

Two years later, and a fortnight after the uproarious Burdon v Rhodes case, Chifney was back at York with Traveller, and a stable-companion, Creeper. Chifney's riding of both horses that week incurred the wrath of the

Baronet, with Sam Chifney up: George Stubbs.

racing fraternity. In both cases he was accused of rank cheating. As the Royal jockey, this was the worst sneer he could face – one which reflected on the Prince of Wales himself.

There were no stewards capable of vindicating Chifney. He was judged, quite understandably, on results. He apparently rode a pathetic race on Traveller, allegedly to get a good match at a good price, and ensured that Creeper flopped by running him into the ground during a training session.

Chifney, who bet quite openly, denied both charges, adding that he had lost two hundred guineas on Creeper. But it seems unlikely that an old hand like Chifney should lose such a sum on the horse which he was riding!

It is possible that money and success had gone to Chifney's head. Although he was subjected to a certain amount of rein from the trainers, it is apparent, from his own statements, that Chifney was very much his own trainer.

One thing seems clear: if Chifney did cheat, he was a cheat among cheats, in days when trickery was much easier, and consequently much more tempting, than it is now. But too many eyes were on Chifney for him to get away with it.

On the Monday of the meeting, Traveller came out against Spadille,

Col. Thornton of Thornville Royal roebuck shooting in the Forest of Glenmore with the only 12-barrelled rifle ever made; Philip Reinagle RA and Sawrey Gilpin RA. (Richard Green Gallery, London)

The Great Match Left to right: *The Earl of Zetland, Voltigeur (Nat Flatman), Robert Hill, Admiral Rous, George Payne, The Flying Dutchman (Charles Marlow), The Earl of Eglinton, John Forbert by J.F. Herring, Snr. (From the Marquis of Zetland's collection)*

The finish of the Great Match which was won by The Flying Dutchman. (York Racing Museum)

Gustavus and Fox in a four-mile race, a common distance in those days. According to Chifney, Traveller, at 4–1, stopped short after two-and-a-quarter miles. Chifney followed the other horses 'as well as I was able', but then thought it prudent to pull Traveller up. 'I now thought Traveller good for nothing, he was beat in such a wonderful way.'

Not very convincing. Chifney claimed that a groom had shown him Traveller shortly after the horse arrived in York. 'I directly observed that he was not fit to run. I sent to inform his Royal Highness that Traveller was not well, and that Creeper was well to run, and I wished his Royal Highness would back Creeper in London,' said Chifney later.

Nevertheless Traveller did run, and on the strength of that performance the owner of Cavendish, a horse which was to race against Traveller later in the week, willingly accepted a match between the two, booked for the following spring at Newmarket.

On Tuesday, the day after Traveller's surprise defeat, Chifney brought both Traveller and Creeper onto Knavesmire for gallops. Creeper was to run in the Great Subscription Race the following day, Wednesday, with Traveller due out again on the Thursday.

Chifney rode Creeper in the gallops, and a small stable boy – 'I think not more than six stones and three pounds' – was on Traveller.

Chifney claimed he told the boy to let Traveller go as well as he was able, and that he, Chifney, simply 'went up to him' on Creeper.

'In my opinion,' Chifney told his critics, 'this running was much less fatigue to Creeper than the gallop he would have had the same morning if he had not run with Traveller.'

After the gallops Chifney learned that Mr W Lake, on behalf of the Prince of Wales, had accepted the Newmarket match for Traveller. According to Chifney, he told Lake that the match was a rash one. Lake replied that if the Prince didn't like to stand the match he would stand every penny himself.

The plot had already thickened when Chifney, on Creeper, was beaten into second place by Walnut in the three-horse race on the Wednesday.

'It was said I lost the race by trying him,' said Chifney. But the gallops, said the Royal jockey, had nothing to do with it. Creeper had been poisoned!

'The instant I had stripped Creeper for saddling, I believed him poisoned for the race, for his carcass was swelled in so extraordinary a manner that I never saw a horse before, and I knew him to have been in fine order only the morning before.'

Had this been so it seems remarkable that the horse ever made the starting post. But Chifney had an answer to this.

'Nothing could now be done for his Royal Highness, and I thought it better for me to lose all my money than to have any complaint made to his Royal Highness that I made the horses wait for me at the starting.'

It is possible that Chifney was riding to instructions, and that reputations were at stake. Success may have gone to his head, but it seems unlikely that he acted entirely independently.

An eighteenth century engraving of York Castle.

By the time Thursday arrived Traveller was 7–1 with Walnut, fresh from his victory the previous day, evens favourite.

Whatever Chifney had originally planned to do in this race, it seems certain that, smarting from so much criticism, he was out to show critics the real Chifney style. Among the field were Gustavus, who had beaten Traveller out of sight on the Monday, and Cavendish, against whom Traveller was to be matched.

The course was the very same that Traveller had run the preceding Monday, but this time Chifney pulled out all the stops. There were six in the field for six-year-olds, and Traveller finished a close third behind Walnut, with 3–1 Tickle Toby the winner. But the main issue was that Traveller had Cavendish well and truly beaten.

At the checking-in Chifney caused a scene by insisting that he had finished second, having to be almost dragged from the scales reserved for the second jockey.

Why this sudden outburst of indignation? Chifney insisted that he hadn't been holding back on the Monday. 'I had the same desire of winning upon Traveller on the first day at York, as I had on any horse,' he protested.

But the critics judged purely on results, and they failed to appreciate how Traveller could be run out of sight by Gustavus on the Monday, yet beat the same horse so convincingly only three days later.

After the race Chifney was approached by a stunned Mr Tyziman, groom to Cavendish, who had been so impressed by Traveller's Monday defeat that, with Cavendish's jockey Thomas Fields, he put fifty guineas on Cavendish to beat Traveller in the Newmarket challenge match.

Would Chifney let them off the bet? Tyziman met a stone wall. 'Tyziman said he knew it was all my making,' said Chifney. 'I told him I had nothing to do about Traveller and Cavendish being matched, neither could I be of any service to him in his bet.'

Chifney expressed surprise that Tyziman should round on him, as he was thinking of recommending Tyziman to the Prince of Wales as a royal groom.

'But after I found that he knew more about me than I knew myself, and seeing him capable of pressing to be off a fifty guinea bet at a time which was so unseasonable, I believed that this sort of conduct was not fit for a Prince's servant.'

Chifney was doubtless glad to get back to Newmarket. But his reputation, earned or otherwise, probably caught up with him. Only two months later he was in trouble again, this time for his riding of Escape, a horse which had been re-purchased by the Prince of Wales.

On October 20 Escape finished last in a race over Newmarket's Ditch Mile. The next day Escape, 5–1 outsider, finished first over the Beacon Course, two miles further.

'The Betting Post' by Rowlandson.

There was a difference of two miles between the race distances, but the Jockey Club stewards spotted a discrepancy in Escape's running. Apart from this, they had been supplied with certain information about Chifney, which was never made public.

Chifney was brought before the Jockey Club and, though nothing could be proved against him, it was made clear that if he ever rode the Prince's horses again no gentleman would start against him. The Prince, not surprisingly, gave up all connections with Newmarket.

The great Chifney still had a lot of racing in him, but he was to ride with the slur on his back. He returned to York for the August meeting of 1800, his arrival at Knavesmire coinciding almost exactly with the hanging there of the pathetic Elizabeth Johnson.

Still the finest jockey of his day, Chifney was now the butt of complaints. If mud were now thrown at him it was pretty certain that most of it would stick. Whatever his record, it is unlikely that Chifney aimed to cheat at this meeting. But he was dogged by his reputation. However, in the days of race matches cheating was rife, and it ill became many of his critics to make Chifney the scapegoat.

He was now riding for a Mr Cookson. His mount was Sir Harry, and Chifney finished last in the two-mile York Oatlands Stakes. Inevitably, one might feel, Chifney was due to ride Sir Harry again the following day. But Cookson was suspicious and, probably with his own reputation in mind, brought in John Singleton, another leading jockey of the day, to replace Chifney.

Rowlandson's picture of Dr Syntax at York races.

The top of a race notice, 1779, showing the finish, grandstand, scales and betting post.

'Mr Cookson took me off Sir Harry, signifying I rode him booty. I did my utmost to win this race with Sir Harry,' claimed Chifney, who blamed Sir Harry's condition. Chifney told Cookson not to think of backing the horse the following day.

Chifney was completely downhearted. Nobody believed a word he spoke. If he didn't win he was suspect. If he finished last he was tried and condemned without defence.

As Chifney was trying to relax overnight in a Dringhouses room, overlooking the course, up came his arch-enemy, Tyziman.

By now Tyziman believed he could treat his peer with contempt. 'Chifney,' he said, 'our north-country gentlemen do not like your way of riding Sir Harry, and they say they will not have such sort of riding here again.'

Chifney told Tyziman he would let Sir Harry speak for him. And it did.

With Singleton up, Sir Harry finished last in a five-horse subscription purse race over four miles.

It was poor comfort for Chifney when Cookson came up to apologise. Chifney had been 'very right' about Sir Harry, said Cookson. But Chifney was still nobody's fool, gaining some solace from having bet 30–20 that Sir Harry would be beaten.

Chifney also took the opportunity of telling Cookson what he thought of his racing contemporaries: 'I told him that I had nearly been sacrificed several times for these last twenty years, and all from these noblemen and gentlemen falling dupes to those cripples who have neither knowledge nor honesty.'

The slanders against Chifney continued throughout what remained of his racing life. He died in Fleet Street lodgings in 1807, leaving a widow and children.

The dawn of a new century saw Chifney's final, sad visit to Knavesmire. But, although his disgrace reflected on the prince he served, Chifney could hardly be accused of a treasonable act ... thank goodness! For Knavesmire had an ominous record of nipping treason in the bud.

8

High Treason
Knavesmire's terrible retribution

Throughout the turmoil of English history Knavesmire served to stamp out any spirit of rebellion among northerners, who detested many of the dictates of a London-based power.

To Yorkshire people, Richard III was the finest of kings – a monarch who loved to visit them, and who had his roots in the county. Bosworth hacked warrior Richard into the mud, paving the way for the usurper Henry Tudor. But Richard lived on in the hearts of Yorkshire folk.

However, feelings were reciprocal, and Henry did not forget that York had sent men to Bosworth to fight at Richard's side.

There was an uprising, led by John Chambers. The Earl of Northumberland, who conveyed the news of Henry's demand for an extra tax to pay for a war in Brittany, was slaughtered. Retribution was swift, and Chambers, termed a 'traitor paramount' was hanged from a specially prepared gibbet which towered above the gallows from which his accomplices hung.

Henry Tudor's son, the awesome Henry VIII, was to be even more sweeping in his use of Knavesmire's 'facilities'.

When Henry ended the Pope's power in England, and closed the monasteries, he met with bitter resistance in the north, where the clergy wished to retain their fundamental allegiance, their way of life, their basic faith and their lands, which would now pass into the hands of southerners.

The drastic closures sparked off a rebellion in the East Riding of Yorkshire and in Lincolnshire. It was led by Robert Aske, a Yorkshire lawyer. Terming themselves 'Pilgrims', the rebels, who included the gallant sixty-two-year-old Lord Hussey and the even older Prior of Bridlington William Wode, courageously protested by restoring sixteen monasteries.

Bearing the banner of the five wounds of Christ, the Pilgrimage of Grace called for the return of papal supremacy. The king, they said, had no cure for souls.

Henry's revenge was ruthless. Lord Hussey was hanged and quartered, the same fate befalling William Wode a month later. A huge crowd turned out to watch Lord Hussey die, shortly after mid-day on August 27, 1537. August was to prove a key month for Knavesmire.

His speech was compelling. He hoped the day was not far away when every Englishman enjoyed the rights and privileges to which he was entitled.

The three-legged mare, York.

His body had hung for twenty minutes when it was cut down for the butchery to begin. He was followed by the abbots of Jervaulx, Rievaulx and Fountains.

What price 'freedom' under Henry VIII? If we cast our eye over the register of freemen for the City of York we see a sickening entry against the name of Valentine Freez, son of a printer: 'Combustus erat apud Knavesmire propter heresem' – 'burned at Knavesmire for heresy'. This was probably at the order of the then Archbishop of York, Edward Lee.

During the reign of the last and greatest of the Tudors, Elizabeth I, the north rebelled again, this time under the leadership of the Earls of Northumberland and Westmorland to release Mary Queen of Scots, restore catholicism and to demand that Elizabeth should recognise Mary as her successor.

The rebellion paid its deathly toll on Knavesmire. Four Yorkshiremen – Simon Digby, John Fulthorpe, Robert Pennyman and Thomas Bishop – had their heads and quarters stuck on the four principal gates into York. Northumberland had escaped, but he was captured two years later and executed.

The end of the divine right of kings, signified by the execution of Charles I, by no means saw the end of injustice.

The aftermath of the Civil War brought retribution on Knavesmire against those who had taken an honourable part in it. The judge who came to York to condemn Colonel John Morris and Lieutenant Blackburn wasn't fit to address them, let alone pass judgment on them.

Morris, a Yorkshireman, had served throughout the war. He changed his convictions, leaving the parliamentary cause to fight for the king. In doing so he made clear his change of colours, but one cannot avoid the suspicion that his change of persuasion had much to do with his subsequent treatment.

He and Blackburn, helped by nine men, captured Pontefract Castle and held out valiantly against the Roundheads' siege. Their ultimate capture led to their appearance before Judge Thorpe, who had conducted a bitter, sweeping and bloody assize that April, during which he extolled the philosophy of the new regime, in an address riddled with invectives against monarchs in general.

At that assize fourteen men were sent to be hanged and quartered on Knavesmire for rebelling against the new establishment. Seven women were hanged too, for a variety of offences.

Morris and Blackburn appeared before Judges Thorpe and Puleston who were specially sent up from London in August to hear the case. The gospel of fear and retribution was a travelling companion. York had stood for the king and it must see the error of its ways.

Colonel Morris produced his appointment, signed by Prince Charles, as governor of Pontefract Castle. His actions, he said, had been governed by the conditions of war. His words fell on deaf ears. In a trial which was a mere formality, he had already been ironed before the verdict was announced. Morris and Blackburn were sentenced to death.

But, as military men, they received military sympathy, a General Lambert having promised them that, whatever the verdict, their lives would be spared if they could escape from York Castle.

On the eve of the execution the pair made their escape bid. At the castle wall Colonel Morris managed to let himself down safely at the other side. But Blackburn, following directly behind him, slipped and broke his leg.

For the second time they had smelled freedom, only for it to be snatched from them. Blackburn urged Morris to carry on without him, but the colonel refused to desert his friend.

They were both easily recaptured, and throughout the remaining hours, before Knavesmire put paid to their aspirations, gave final testimony of their loyalty. They were condemned in a city which had proclaimed loyalty to

The Knavesmire gallows.

King Charles during the war, a city whose walls had been blasted by the Roundhead bombardments.

Yesterday's friends, today's enemies; today's enemies, yesterday's friends; retribution, counter-retribution – the pattern would not change. The restoration of the monarchy brought an all-too-familiar situation.

Charles II was at first unpopular with many of his subjects, who objected to the licentiousness of the new court. Conspiracy was widespread, but rebellion, quite typically you might think, came to a head only in Yorkshire.

At the root of it were ex-roundhead soldiers and preachers, who aimed to seize garrisons in the north and arrest leading members of royalty. They wanted a change in government, tithes to be scrapped and bishops put out of office. There had to be a widespread reformation, particularly among lawyers and clergymen.

Yet again did Knavesmire nip ill-advised, ill-prepared rebellion in the bud. Poorly armed, the rebels allowed their plans to be an open secret. Overwhelmed by regular soldiers, they were treated with the utmost severity. Another special commission was sent up from London – this time in the depths of winter.

Eighteen were hanged and quartered on Knavesmire, their limbs being conspicuously placed at various points along the city's walls and fortifications – the same fortifications which had withstood the king's enemies during the civil war.

How wise it was to be a Stuart supporter then, but how unwise after Bonnie Prince Charlie's ill-fated uprising.

When Highlander won the opening race at the York August meeting of 1748, the fields of Culloden still heard the cries of the wounded Highlanders, who had been bayoneted to death two years previously.

Culloden ended a dream – the dream of The Young Pretender to restore the throne to the Stuarts, and to take it from that Hanoverian, the very king who gave his patronage to the York race which Highlander was to win.

On his way back from Culloden, the Duke of Cumberland, commander of His Majesty's Forces, known more pertinently as 'Butcher' Cumberland, stopped in York, where he was given a tremendous welcome, a banquet and the freedom of the city. Cumberland stayed overnight in a riverside street, which was re-named in his honour. In return for the hospitality which he had received, Cumberland left behind a batch of Culloden prisoners.

Before the judges opened the assize they attended the traditional service in York, where the high sheriff's chaplain read out an appropriate message: 'And the Lord said unto Moses, "Take all the heads of the people and hang them up before the sun"'. Heads would, indeed, be put on display.

With the Lord now being introduced to back the Hanoverian cause, the prisoners had little hope of clemency. Of the seventy-five who were tried, seventy were sentenced to death. However, of these only twenty-three were executed, the remainder being transported or, provided they enlisted, pardoned.

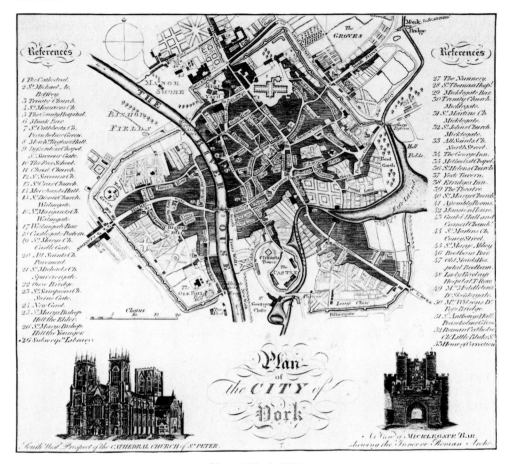

Plan of York 1820.

Among the condemned was a piper, James Reid from Angus, whose defence argued that, as he had never carried arms and had never struck a blow against the king's men, James should be spared.

The jury recommended mercy, but Lord Chief Baron Parker would have none of it: 'No regiment ever marched without musical instruments, and a Highland regiment never marched without a piper; therefore his bagpipe, in the eyes of the law, is a weapon of war', he ruled.

As the sledges grated and bumped their way up Castlegate on the way to Knavesmire, a royal messenger galloped up to bring glad tidings of a reprieve for one of the sad cargo – John James Fellens, who must have been in a sick daze as he was taken from his sledge and led back to the castle.

The ritual at Knavesmire had not become refined with the passage of time. When the condemned had hung for ten minutes their bodies were cut down and stripped before the butchery began.

The heads of two were carried back along the death route, to be stuck on the ramparts of Micklegate Bar – the very gateway which had borne the skull of Richard, Duke of York, during the Wars of the Roses.

The second, final batch of Culloden's defeated were dealt with a week later. The last to die was a young piper, without the likes of whom no Highland regiment was complete.

There was racing as usual that year, while the heads of Bonnie Prince Charlie's men still adorned that formidable gateway into the city.

Horses of death conveying their cartloads of doom to the gallows; horses of life clumping their way round the damp, often soggy four-mile route to the grandstand – this was to be the way of things until the Three-legged Mare claimed its last victim, Edward Hughes, in 1801.

While Hyperion, a name to be borne with fame by a twentieth century horse, was being nudged into second place by Hippopotumus in the Great Produce Stakes of 1797, Robert Dawson, a highly-esteemed postmaster from Bawtry, near Doncaster, was awaiting his execution on Knavesmire. Just after the meeting ended, Dyson was hanged for embezzling a bill and destroying a letter.

York Castle from a print of 1728.

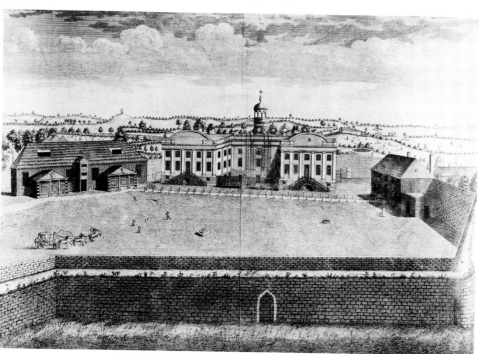

71

Short of cash, he had hoped to make good his deception later. His neighbours came to see him die – not through vulgar curiosity, but to pay their last respects. His widow and daughter maintained their standards in Bawtry by opening a glass and china shop there.

In 1802 the morbid had a new meeting place – directly outside the castle walls, to where the gallows had now been transferred. They had a gala eleven years later when the Luddite rioters went to their deaths there.

By 1868, when the death sentence had already been restricted to the crimes of murder and treason, the place of execution was inside the prison – a 'drop' replacing the older method of strangulation.

Now York races were free of that shadow, which had been cast over the course for seventy years. If the reputation of the racing were to be redeemed, then surely this must be the time. But it was not to be.

For the very notoriety of Knavesmire, its 'dual role', had proved an inducement. There seems little doubt that the gallows had, indirectly, proved a hideous benefit to the races, as well as a curse.

The racing, such as it was, now stood out in stark relief, like a ballroom in the aftermath of a prolonged dance of debauchery. The gallows had gone, yes, but York races had a period of attrition to undergo before they were to be redeemed. A deep stain is not removed speedily.

In the meantime, there were the uproarious moments, of course. Life cannot be tragic all the time. Challenge matches, often used to settle personal feuds, provided much speculation and entertainment, particularly when the protagonists took themselves seriously.

They provided a meeting place for some of the most noteworthy eccentrics in the history of the English Turf – for men, and women, who lived in a distinct world of their own, in which rules were bent like reeds and hats flung high.

Yes, challenge matches were the disorder of the day. But, for the perfect ingredients, we need that little touch of scandal. Take two jealous, arrogant men; spice with a daring, delectable lady jockey and the result is a most entertaining dish . . .

9

Alicia Thornton's grand challenges

 There once was a girl called Alicia, desribed in a contemporary observation as fascinating, but somewhat lacking in 'pretty virginities'. Fascinating she certainly was, her attractiveness and compelling personality leaving hysterical excitement and near-catastrophe in their wake.

Daughter of a Norwich watchmaker, Alicia Meynell certainly had a keen sense of timing – fast enough for any horseman of her day, and probably a little too fast for a certain Colonel Thomas Thornton, of Thornville Royal, near Knaresborough.

Alicia was twenty-two when she met the colonel, who was obviously captivated by her competitive spirit, as well as by her other attributes. Despite the apparent restriction of the side-saddle style of riding, Alicia was more than a match for most male competitors, and was anxious to prove that she was better than the best.

Her alliance with Colonel Thornton was to prove the key to the fulfilment of her ambition. The alliance, indeed, provided interest in itself, the eyebrows of 1804 raising themselves in unison when Alicia began to ride under the name of Mrs Thornton.

The colonel was a likely candidate for the job. A man with an eye for the unusual he had the brilliant idea of letting wolves loose in the tranquil Yorkshire Wolds so that he could hunt them – an aspiration which astounded even the most eccentric of his contemporaries. Much to the relief of all villagers concerned, he was talked into restricting himself to fox-hunting. He was, however, considered a leading light in the sporting world, being the proud possessor of a vast array of all types of hounds, as well as an extensive stable.

So here they were – the daring, delectable horsewoman and her champion. To complete the picture a protagonist was needed. He surfaced in the shape of Captain Flint, celebrated sportsman and 'scientific' angler – the word 'scientific' appearing to have distinctly mysterious connotations.

Fully backed by the colonel, Alicia stunned the racing world by challenging Flint to a four-mile match on Knavesmire for five hundred guineas, with a thousand guineas bye. So outlandish was this intrusion into the male domain that more attention was lavished on the challenge than on the rest of contemporary Turfing activities combined.

On the day of the race York was simmering with speculation. Many thousands had ridden, or walked, to the city overnight, from both town and country. Business boomed for publicans, showmen and touts. Betting was intense, but much of it was frivolous. Most people were concerned that Alicia should either win – or lose. Flint was simply representing the male gender.

By four o'clock a carpet of people covered Knavesmire, observers estimating the crowd at nearly a hundred thousand.

Alicia made her grand entrance, led in by a proud, expectant Colonel Thornton, who was basking in the glory of this newly-acquired publicity. Alicia's dress for the occasion appears to have been tasteful, practical, but eye-catching. She sported a jockey cap, silk blouse and the long, sweeping skirt which was then in vogue.

Many a male heart fluttered as the watchmaker's daughter awaited the time for off.

She was riding the colonel's chestnut Vinagrillio against Captain Flint's brown Thornville. Whether bad feeling existed between Thornton and Flint is questionable; but it certainly made itself evident afterwards.

Alicia held the lead for the first three miles, in a style described by her admirers as 'masterly'. But, with just under a mile to go, her horse fell lame, and Flint triumphantly took over the lead. Realising that it was impossible for her to win, Alicia pulled up Vinagrillio, who staggered gamely home, the crowd acknowledging the lady's sportsmanlike behaviour. Male chauvinism, many were pleased to say, had been preserved.

Alicia, who knew full well that she was more than a match for Flint, was already angry when she saw a reference to the race in the *Yorkshire Herald*. Her complexion deepened to a gentle shade of purple as she read of how the 'beautiful heroine' had been paid every attention by the captain.

Enough was enough! The editor concerned walked with wary step, justifiably dreading the sudden appearance of an Alicia out for his blood. A letter from the lady scorched a patch on his desk. Alicia denied that she had been allowed any consideration at all. Flint, in fact, had been downright rude, treating her as an outsider in every sense of the word. He had told her to 'keep to that side Ma'am'. This would have been fine for a morning's social canter, but was hardly appropriate for a needle match.

But Alicia then made the mistake of claiming that she was entitled to special consideration, on account of her sex: 'When my horse broke down in the terrible way he did, all the course must have witnessed the handsome way in which Mr Flint brought me in. He left me out, by distancing me as much as he possibly could. If these should be received as precedents, the art of riding against ladies will be made most completely easy.'

Emotions were beginning to run high, and it is not difficult to guess why. Thornton, Flint and Alicia were involved in a little drama, which developed into melodrama by the time it reached Knavesmire. Almost certainly, Flint visited Thornville Royal, his visits there increasing appreciably after the

York Meeting

The Celebrated Race between Mr Thornton's Vingarillo & Mr Flint's br: h. Thornville
which was run for on Knavesmire Augt 25 1804 — A Match for 500 gs. & 1000 gs. bye Four Miles.
London Publish'd by R.^t Cribb Junr N.º 288. High Holborn

The celebrated race between Captain Flint and Mrs Thornton, 1804.

arrival of Alicia. One imagines that, in pre-Alicia days, Colonel Thomas Thornton and Flint were on amicable terms, and that they went riding together in the grounds of Thornville.

The trouble started when the riding party numbered three, Flint falling hopelessly for Alicia – a condition which he strove to disguise behind a jolly, sporting mask of male self-assertion. Women know this ploy of old, and Alicia must have been confident that Flint would accept her challenge. Thornton, who liked a bit of chasing, but without the racing, probably felt a little insecure and, consequently, jealous.

He was proud of his Alicia and he would prove it, both to her and to the world, by being her champion. Doubtless Flint and Alicia had several furious little matches up at Thornville before the female gauntlet was finally flung down. And the horse that Flint rode at York, Thornville, obviously belonged to the colonel.

Alicia, therefore, was confident of victory, and would probably have romped home had her horse not broken down. A gloating, condescending

Captain Flint made defeat all the more bitter. 'I did not expect Mr Flint to shake hands with me – that, I understand, being the common prelude to boxing,' she protested.

But Alicia was not going to let the matter rest at that. The result of the match was not at all conclusive, and a re-match was essential. 'After all this', Alicia told the *Yorkshire Herald*, 'I challenge Mr Flint to ride the same match, in all its terms, over the same course next year.'

The affair was providing great entertainment value, with poems and songs being devoted to the romantic feud between the Thorntons and Flint, whose attitude to the return bout was thus penned in verse:

> *To your challenge anew I beg to reply,*
> *When your ladyship's made every bet,*
> *I'll be proud to attend, the contest to try,*
> *For the honour again of your wit.'*

Pretty, Alicia undoubtedly was, but there is little evidence that she was particularly witty. The passionate trio were to provide a certain unconscious humour, but the mood, as far as they were concerned, was changing rapidly.

The colonel couldn't, or wouldn't, settle his account with Flint over the first match, so Flint, quite naturally, refused the re-match. The reasonably good-natured rivalry that had existed between the two now deteriorated into a quarrel, with most of Yorkshire taking sides.

The row came to a head at York's summer meeting the following year. Captain Flint was, by now, thoroughly infuriated by the colonel's refusal to hand over that one thousand pounds – a sum the enormity of which the colonel fully appreciated. Alicia was proving not only decidedly expensive, but also particularly shrewd, leaving the two of them to bang their rather dense heads together while she got on with her own plans.

It was the Thursday, and the crowd in front of the grandstand was milling around quite amiably – chatting, gossiping, flirting, puzzling out how to find the best debauch for the evening, or simply taking an interest in the racing – when in stormed an extremely flinty Flint. Ignoring the astonished gathering, Flint strode over to one of the wooden pillars, whipped an ominous piece of paper from his pocket, nailed it home and stalked away. The crowd hurried forward, craning their necks to read the announcement. It was about Colonel Thornton: 'pay up, pay up and play the game'. Speculation about the outcome was to provide food enough for the evening's enjoyment. And the following day, the colonel obliged by turning up at the races.

Time for the showdown, and Flint was ready – not with another piece of paper, but with a horse-whip! Now for that Thornton fellow.

Whatever Thornton expected, it wasn't this. Women gasped in slightly feigned horror, and men protested indignantly as Flint laid into the colonel with great vigour. Poor Flint. He had almost certainly lost the lady of his affections, and now, by losing his temper before a gathering with a substantial female representation, he was losing whatever support he had enjoyed.

A contemporary caricature of the race.

The crowd greeted his idiotic outburst with hissing and booing. Among them was the Lord Mayor, who hadn't come to watch this, and a number of city magistrates, who were indignant about being called upon to perform their tedious duty. This they did, however, turning upon one or two of the city runners and ordering them to 'arrest that man'.

At this point we can take a look at the profit and loss account of the business which started with those flirtatious canterings through the grounds of Thornville Royal. The captain, who has won a race for a thousand pounds, which he will never receive, has also lost the lady whose affections he was craving, and against whom he raced in the first place. In addition, he is thrown into jail, until he can find one thousand pounds – the amount which he has won, but will never receive, from the challenge match. He must also find sureties from two other people. Apart from that, the affair has been a resounding success.

The colonel's situation is quite different. He has managed to champion a lady, who has proved a distinct drain on his purse. His pride has been dented through Alicia's defeat. He has, most assuredly, squabbled with Alicia and has been publicly denounced as a man who does not honour his debts. He has also been bound over to prosecute Flint, which could prove an embarrassment. Last, but not least, he has an extremely sore back.

A commemorative goblet of Mrs Thornton's challenge, which is in the racing museum at Knavesmire.

But what of our 'femme fatale'? While the two chaps were busy making fools of themselves, Alicia had her mind fixed on her priority – to prove that she was more than a match for the best jockey in the land. The return match with Flint had fallen through. The inimitable Alicia went one better, challenging none other than the renowned Frank Buckle, master jockey of the day, to a match at Knavesmire in the August.

Alicia was to ride Louisa, owned by the ever-suffering colonel, with Buckle on Allegro, owned by Mr Bloomfield. The match was for a gold cup worth seven hundred guineas; the distance two miles.

One can fully appreciate the enormous interest that this confrontation aroused, and many thousands hoofed or trod their way to York, filling the inns overnight. Some slept in hedgerows, some on wood, some in beds. Many never bothered to sleep at all.

Louisa was carrying nine stones and six pounds, and Allegro thirteen stones and six pounds – a slight disparity, one is forced to observe. Nevertheless, the handicap must have been viewed as reasonable by all the parties involved.

Alicia managed to emphasise her comeliness by turning out in a purple cap and waistcoat, nankeen-coloured skirts, purple shoes and embroidered stockings. She went straight into the lead, which she maintained for an appreciable time. Buckle, wisely, held back his challenge. He drew level with Alicia, then passed her, and for a few lengths it looked as though his experience would be the deciding factor.

But no! Back came Alicia, drawing level as the winning post loomed enticingly near. The crowd bordered on the delirious as Louisa strained across the line, half a neck in front of Allegro. Now, truly, was Alicia the heroine, as Louisa sauntered back through rows of beaming faces. No-one was condescending now, as congratulations rang through the air. No-one, that is, apart from a bunch of Buckle supporters.

These gentlemen were having their own private sulk. Alicia, they claimed, had taken unfair advantage of their champion. Her dress was so outrageous that it had scared Buckle's horse, causing it not to run properly. Even Allegro, apparently, had a crush on Alicia. This, we should all have witnessed. To be fair to Buckle himself, he is not on record as subscribing to such an idiotic assertion.

Alicia had now, well and truly, made her point. Having done so, she disappeared from the York scene leaving a trail of chaos.

Flint and Thornton were whizzing around rapidly getting nowhere. In the presence of the colonel, Flint appealed to the Jockey Club at York, possibly represented by the stewards of the meeting.

Thornton then lost any support he had by claiming that Flint's bet on the race had been 'a sham'. Its aim had been to attract attention, even acclaim, and the admiring company that such fame enticed. 'You deserved to be horsewhipped Thornton', raged one of the stewards. A halo suddenly appeared above the head of Captain Flint as the stewards turned towards him as one man and chorused: 'Give him another if he doesn't pay up'.

But the colonel went on and on, refusing to climb down from a ladder which was on the point of collapse. The case came before Lord Ellenborough

Rowlandson's cartoon of Dr Syntax on his way to the races.

in the High Court, who also grew rapidly fed up with Thornton. If he, the colonel, had thought it appropriate, in the first place, to apply to the Jockey Club, he had no justification for an appeal to the High Court. If he so wished, he could go before a grand jury.

Thornton probably would have done so, but for one small matter – money, or lack of it. At this time he was in what are euphemistically termed 'reduced financial circumstances'. Only a year later he was forced to sell Thornville Royal and the estate to Lord Stourton, moving to Spye Park in Wiltshire. A decade passed before he left for France, where he died in 1823, aged seventy-five.

Poor Flint fared even worse. That victory on Knavesmire was a Pyrrhic one indeed. Elusive Alicia was elsewhere, and they had never had that return match. If she had won that one, he could have challenged her. He would certainly have won the following one, then she could have challenged him again, and they could have gone on and on, challenging and counter-challenging into a magical eternity. But it wasn't to be. Flint went down and down, dissipating all his property while Alicia, oblivious to his condition, was almost certainly enjoying life with somebody else.

He became prey to asthmatic attacks, which he counteracted with repeated doses of prussic acid. One bitterly-cold morning in January, 1832, he took so large a dose of the horrible stuff that it caused his death.

Farewell to the devastating trio. Short-lived though their relationship was, it never lapsed into tedium. It was far too insecure for that.

10

Some notable Knavesmire eccentrics

 Knavesmire, in its pre-renaissance days, never lacked eccentrics. There was, for example, the inimitable Lord March, who attended York races for half a century, and who consistently bore the characteristics of the March hare.

He loved challenges, and was responsible in the eighteenth century for inaugurating matches on Knavesmire. In one of them he rode his own horse, Whipper-in, to victory.

The third Earl of March, however, was better known for his tendency to do exactly as he pleased without caring whom he offended, or whom he involved. Above all, he delighted in showing that he could perform the impossible.

Ridiculous bets were the result, and there was always someone around with sufficient money, and insufficient sense, to accept a wager. A notable example was his claim that he could send a letter fifty miles within an hour. No, he didn't use a complicated relay of sprinting horses, a string of archers or a series of paperweight guns. It was far more subtle than that.

He strolled up to a group of cricketers, who were waiting for their turn to bat in a village match, and told them, if their team and the opposition would turn up at Knavesmire a few days later, and help him win a little wager, he would stand them ale for the night. 'You're on!' To men who loved the sound of ball on bat there was only one note sweeter – the gurgling of beer as the pewter welcomed its release from the barrel. Whether those teams had a twelfth man or not is uncertain, but they certainly had for this fixture. Twenty-four players turned up, all suffering from dry throats.

Up strode March with a cricket ball in his hand. But this ball was different; it had a hole in it. 'Stand in a circle please, not too close together,' said March. Following his instructions, the cricketers gawped in bewilderment as he paced out the distance between them. He then walked to the centre of the circle, mumbling calculations as he did so. He then took a letter from his pocket – a proper one, which was addressed to the bemused folk who had accepted the wager. The letter said, in effect, 'Told you so'.

Now for the grand finale. March crammed the letter into the hole in the ball, threw it to one of the players and said: 'When I call "go" I want to see that ball flying round the ring as fast as possible. Don't stop until I tell you.'

STORRY's LIST.——YORK SPRING MEETING, 1798.

TUESDAY, May 22.

MR. G. Crompton's bay colt, Honeycomb, by Drone, *received forfeit from* Mr. Clifton's bay colt, Agriculture, by Farmer, dam by Young Marſk, for 100gs. each,

Top of the race card, spring meeting 1798.

Off went the ball on its merry-go-round, with March settling himself in a seat which had been brought out for him. The rhythm became painfully monotonous as March, watch in hand, kept note of the laps, balancing distance travelled against time in hand.

'Faster, faster,' he cried in desperation, as the weary players, reproaching themselves bitterly for being such idiots, bore distinct signs of flagging. Whatever game this was, it just wasn't cricket. The zany earl, incidentally, had failed to take a significant point into consideration.

Cricket teams then, as now, contained a sprinkling of left-arm bowlers. Many a right-hand batsman threw the ball left-handed, and March's twenty-four misguided helpers were as well balanced a group of chaps as you could meet. The ball was fizzing round in a clockwise direction, setting no problems for the earl's calculations until it found the hands of a left-hander.

March groaned each lap as the luckless fellow had to pivot a full one hundred and eighty degrees before the ball could continue on its journey. 'For God's sake,' exclaimed the eccentric earl, 'put someone else in there'. There was no-one else, he was informed. 'Then tell him to drop out.'

With much relief the left-hander followed instructions. This farce had been going on for more than half an hour, and one man fewer in the line-up wouldn't make much difference anyway. The remaining twenty-three kept the ball rolling, mesmerised by its monotonous magic. This particular cricket ball was no longer an ordinary one: it was starting to sing a little song. They all joined in the singing of what soon developed into a sea-shanty. 'That's the spirit lads,' roared the now exuberant March, who smelled success in the air. His watch was ticking much more merrily.

Throats were no longer dry, they were parched. Some people will do anything for a drink, but these fellows had exceeded the call of duty. 'Stop!' The earl leapt to his feet exuberantly. 'We've done it!'

The cricketers stood transfixed as March raced round them, vigorously shaking right hands which seemed to have lost all touch with reality and all sense of touch.

March was true to his word, and the ale flowed that evening, every gallant cricketer raising his left-arm to toast the earl who made it all possible. Everyone, that is, apart from the left-hander, who raised his right arm in tribute.

March devoted his life to the Turf, to fine wines, to the fine arts and to those impossible schemes of his. Without the benefit of modern medical advice, he died in 1810, aged eighty-six.

The challenge matches that he had inaugurated at York began to swamp the racing calendar. On one day in 1771 there were no fewer than five. Frequently the challenges were rash ones, made after too much socialising, or out of a misguided sense of bravado. Rich owners frequently thought twice, withdrawing their horses at the last moment. At one meeting alone four forfeits were handed over. Typical was one of two hundred and fifty guineas and a hogshead of claret, paid by Sir Dundas Pontac to a Mr Fenwick.

Subscription races, such as the farcical one which resulted in the Burdon v Rhodes case, were also common, but rarely a feast for the racing gourmet. Many owners concerned in these galloping get-togethers rode their own horses. Leading members of various hunts, they regarded their private little races as annual reunions of old chums. Winner takes all, and claret all round. We can see what old one-eyed Kitty Rowntree was up against.

But let us give credit to these men, without whom racing at York would not have survived at all. Their allegiances were to God, the King and the Turf, in that order.

They were creatures, too, of habit, with a distinct tint of licentiousness. During racing week many of them found creature comforts at the Black Swan in Coney Street – a thoroughfare which bustles now just as much as it did in those days of the stage-coach. Affectionately known as the Black Duck or Mucky Duck, it was as the Black Duck that it lent its name to the Black Duck Stakes, one of the longest running of York's subscription races. The last one was run in 1870, the death of one of its principal subscribers, Lord Glasgow, spelling the end of such events on Knavesmire.

James Boyle, fifth Earl of Glasgow and the Mucky Duck – what a combination that was!

When we dine out, we express displeasure at poor service or food in varying ways – by complaining, insisting that the offending inedible item be replaced, or by being thoroughly miserable for the rest of the evening, vowing never to darken that doorstep again. Lord Glasgow, however, had every intention of darkening that doorstep again and again. If he chose to stay at the Black Swan, then that inn had better adapt itself to his whims. He

The Black Swan Hotel.

was not going to stop losing his temper on their account.

What exactly the poor waiter did, or didn't do, at the Mucky Duck one certain evening during race week in the 1840s is a little unclear. It is likely, however, that the chap made the mistake of existing within arm's length of the crusty peer while Glasgow was in one of his foul moods. Possibly the fifth course was having an internal battle with the fourth.

The result was that the waiter found himself floating straight through the window, which was fortunately open. It was even more fortunate for the waiter concerned that it occurred on the ground floor. The innkeeper, to give the man his due, was sufficiently concerned to point out to the volcanic Glasgow that his latest eruption would prove rather costly. The waiter concerned did not possess an insurance policy which covered such mishaps. Fingers scorched by hot plates, yes; clothing stained by spilled broth, yes; but broken limbs incurred through reaching the street by the most direct route, definitely no.

'All right, what's the cost?', queried a far-from-repentant Glasgow, who whatever his faults, prided himself on paying his dues. 'Let's say five pounds', ventured the innkeeper, glancing nervously towards the window, and praying that he would not follow the waiter's airborne route. 'Put it on the bill,' snapped Glasgow. The innkeeper obliged, featuring the item among the sundries: 'Breaking waiter's arm – five pounds!'

Glasgow could be equally liverish over liver – animal liver that is. The next time we find him in one of his charming moods at the Mucky Duck is over breakfast. Life lost its meaning for him when his customary calf's liver, which invariably formed a partnership with bacon, failed to materialise. Steam began to filter through Glasgow's ears, and the waiter concerned, not wishing to be added to the bill at the end of the week, sought the comparative cool of the kitchen.

'Not his flaming Lordship again!' The innkeeper looked despairingly to the ceiling, but could find no calf's liver there. In fact, there was no calf's liver anywhere. He had scoured the city for calf's liver. He had been up and down the Shambles – that ancient, narrow street which groaned with meat of every description – begging all the butchers to find just a little calf's liver. Well, there was plenty of ox-liver, some nice pig's liver (out of the question) and what would his Lordship think to a little bit of lamb's liver? His thoughts would be unrepeatable.

This was one of Lord Glasgow's high-level complaints and only the innkeeper could deal with it. Bracing himself for action, and with the good wishes of his staff accompanying him, he approached Glasgow's table.

The 5th Earl of Glasgow.

'Where's my calf's liver?' Glasgow's temper was matched only by his eloquence. The landlord, wishing that someone, some day, would stuff Glasgow into a tub of calf's liver and drop it into the Ouse, explained the situation. 'In short, your Lordship, there is not a single piece of calf's liver in the city.'

'Then, damn it, why don't you go somewhere and buy a calf?', thundered Glasgow. And he wasn't joking. Glasgow was not noted for his wit, and whatever jokes featured in his repertoire, they would not concern such a serious subject as breakfast without calf's liver.

He was not devoid of generosity, however, having a certain philanthropic attitude towards old people in particular. During race nights he and his friends would hand out tumblers of claret to the elderly as they passed by the Black Swan. The only snag with this was that the recipients didn't like claret, being used to the beverage that surrounded them – ale. In any case, a square meal would have gone down far better. Many a tumbler was furtively emptied into the street.

Lord Glasgow was not the only Mucky Duck regular to demand slavish attention. Take old Sir Tatton Sykes, for example, a racing stalwart without whom no York meeting was complete.

Every year Sir Tatton rode the twenty-four miles from his Sledmere home to the inn, and every year everything was in its place, just as it should be. The Black Swan became even more of a home from home when it was taken over by Mr and Mrs Hussey, who had been butler and cook to him at Sledmere. So he was always assured of the best at the Mucky Duck.

If 'Owd' Sir Tatton happened to turn up late, then the inn, somehow, had to adapt itself to the situation. So when, one year, he and his servant trotted into the coach-yard long after they were due, Sir Tatton's mind devoted itself purely to the luxury which undoubtedly awaited him.

But, for once, the world had forgotten where Sir Tatton was, or should be. In fact, during the hectic scramble which invariably took place at the inn on the eve of race week – rooms, beds, meals, coaches – Sir Tatton had been forgotten altogether.

'Look who's here!' exclaimed Mr Hussey. His wife hurried to the window, and looked down into the coach-yard. 'Oh no!' she groaned, 'I didn't think he was coming.' She rushed down into the yard, a flurry of petticoats and apologies: 'I really didn't know you were coming . . . I know you always like that particular room but, well, I'm ever so sorry Your Lordship, but, well, I've had to let it to somebody else . . . you know what it's like, race week and all . . . but don't you worry, I've got some other rooms free, much nicer than the one you usually stay in.'

The pause seemed to last an eternity. Ostler, servant, Mrs Hussey – all looked up expectantly at Sir Tatton, who stayed impassively in the saddle. Surely he couldn't reject such an offer, made so sweetly. Eventually the reply rasped down: 'Mrs Hussey, you're a hussy!' Beckoning his servant to follow, he then turned his horse and trotted from the yard – all the way back to

Sir Tatton Sykes (left) *at Sledmere.*

Sledmere. He was, most assuredly, cutting off his nose to spite his face for, as a result of his tantrum, he missed the entire meeting.

But Sir Tatton had plenty of time to reflect on his error, and next year he was back at the Mucky Duck . . . on time.

York was always conscious of its racecourse, dubious though the quality of racing frequently was, and by the middle of the eighteenth century, when the Race Committee began to take stock of its deficiencies, the influence of the Turf was pictured on the signs that hung from the inns – Eclipse, Bloomsbury, Bee's Wing, Marcia, Charles II and a profusion of Horse and Jockeys.

But the York Tavern smelled more turfy than any of them. Bookmakers were not yet in business, so both noblemen and commoners crammed into a room at the tavern during race week to wager between themselves. Pipe-smoke filled the air and smocked waiters hurried backwards and forwards with trays of drink as politics, news and gossip were exchanged.

It was here that a party of noblemen, headed by Lord Fitzwilliam, decided to stay the night, after a heavy bout of eating and drinking during the 1796 meeting. Judging by the quantity that the thirty consumed between them, they would have had little alternative but to stay in the tavern. It's doubtful if many of them managed to stagger to their feet.

To soak up the wide variety of beverages which they guzzled, they ate ruffs and reeves – rather uncommon wading birds, apart from being delicacies. The liquid they poured down continually changed, both in colour and character and, after an hour or so of this treatment, it is unlikely that their palates had even the remotest idea of what they were being called upon to savour.

Their bill for the evening, which must have seen in the dawn, came to thirty-two pounds and fifteen shillings and included hock, gin, lemon and sugar, malt liquor, madeira, lemonade, Bristol water, brandy, claret, sherry, port, seltzer water, tea and coffee. A fascinating, mixed aperitif, to give that little edge to breakfast a few hours later.

Was anyone ever going to restore the tone of racing in York, or were we forever going to have this succession of farces and debaucheries? Fear not, gallantry had not totally disappeared. Here comes the cavalry to the rescue, in the shape of the 2nd Dragoon Guards.

In 1822 these gentlemen racked their brains to find a way of raising the tone at York. They winced at recalling an observation, made only a few years previously by someone who had casually called in at the races: 'I was pressed on all sides; a belle had passed her fine hand round my neck, and another thrust her velvet cheek past mine, unmindful of what they did, for the great business was to see what was passing below.' It is convenient, for the purposes of maintaining the tone of our story, to pass a veil over what was happening below.

The officers of the 2nd Dragoons aimed to put an end to this nonsense. So, with the full co-operation of an equally concerned Race Committee, they introduced an extra meeting to the calendar, the Craven meeting, which was to provide entertaining racing for true gentlemen.

It seemed a cracking idea at the time, and the chaps from the Dragoons received full support from members of the neighbouring hunts. The plans were foolproof, and the first Craven meeting took place in 1823, the opening race being, appropriately, the Craven Stakes, 'a race for gentlemen riders only, over one-and-a-quarter miles.'

A horse called Tom Paine, owned by a certain Mr Rowlay, was the winner, going on to win the Hunters' Stakes, for horses not thoroughbred, later in the afternoon, at odds of 5-2.

But the 2nd Dragoons, and the Race Committee, were in for a nasty shock. For it was discovered, two years later, that 'Tom Paine' was none other than a horse called Tybalt, which had been having a successful career under its true name – so successful indeed that our Mr Rowlay decided to run it under a different one. The poor old 2nd Dragoons had succeeded in putting Knavesmire's clock back. But this time the winner of a highly-esteemed race for gentlemen only was certainly not a gentleman.

Mr Rowlay must have had a hide as thick as that of a rhinoceros, for he turned up at Knavesmire with Tybalt, alias Tom Paine, only weeks after his masquerade had been discovered. To add insult to injury he was putting 'Tom Paine' against Bogtrotter (a race involving the two having led to the revelation of Tom Paine's true identity).

This Tom was certainly proving a pain for York races. Shortly before the race was due to start a steward walked up to Rowlay and told him he was not to race: 'We have had an objection that your horse is not a half-bred, but the thoroughbred Tybalt, formerly the property of Lord Grosvenor, and not bred, as you have certified, by yourself.'

An investigation was held at Knavesmire the following morning, at the end of which Rowlay was told to prove the pedigree of Tom Paine within a month. Meanwhile, it could not be entered in any races for half-breds. The astonishing thing is that the stewards allowed the horse to compete as Tybalt.

The Jockey Club's suspicions were confirmed. Rowlay could produce no certificate for 'Tom Paine', and the horse was disqualified from every race in which it had participated under that name. Regarding the race which had been due to take place at York, the money was given to Bogtrotter's owner and all bets declared void.

Poor old 2nd Dragoons, and their well-laid plans. They didn't even have the satisfaction of seeing Rowlay and his accomplices warned off. As for Tom Paine, we find him winning a race up in Scotland the following September, under the ownership of a Mr Lewis.

But 1825 wasn't a complete disaster, a ray of light piercing the gloom in the form of the new Great Yorkshire Stakes, to be won by Cymbeline.

The general standard of racing on Knavesmire was, however, proving notable only for its mediocrity. Indeed, the spring meeting of 1828 was so uninspiring that racegoers looked to the cockpits for their week's entertainment. A new pit had been built next to the Assembly Rooms, together with a betting room and club-house for race subscribers.

Most of the betting that week was on the cockfighting – a grand main between Sir Bellingham Graham and Henry Wormald forming the opening encounter in the new pit. Blood and feathers flew throughout the evenings of Monday to Thursday. Sir Bellingham, whose horse, The Duchess, had won the St Leger of 1816, was easily beaten. The reason was that his birds were suffering from the highly-contagious poultry disease known as roup, caused generally by bad feeding, housing or ventilation.

The birds should either have been isolated or killed. But Sir Bellingham, sportsman that he was, allowed them to go out fighting, almost certainly passing on the disease to the opposition in the process.

This, then, was the scene at the Assembly Rooms – a far cry from the days of Rockingham. Society was steering clear of the assemblies which, for years, had lost their priority in many a diary. Indeed, so critical had the situation become that the Yorkshire Union Hunt Club members were concerned as much about the Assembly Rooms as they were about the standard of racing.

C. ABBOTT
(Late "SCAWIN"),
RAIL WAY AND FAMILY HOTEL,
(FIRST CLASS)
YORK.

Established many years. Refurnished and thoroughly renovated. Adjoining the Station Gates. The largest Hotel in York. Private Rooms. Ladies' and Gentlemen's Coffee Rooms. Every accommodation for Night Travellers. Porters attend the Station night and day. A good commercial connection attached to this house. Excellent Stabling. Brilliant Saloon.

N.B.—ASK FOR ABBOTT'S PORTERS.

YORK.
BLACK SWAN HOTEL,

CONEY STREET.

This is the only exclusively *Family Hotel*, centrally situated, Winn's "George Hotel" having been pulled down.

This old-established COUNTY HOTEL has been entirely renovated and newly furnished, and, as a FIRST-CLASS HOTEL, affords unexceptionable accommodation for Private Families and Tourists, being in the immediate vicinity of the Railway, Post Office, Cathedral, Assembly Rooms, and the ruins of St. Mary's Abbey. AMERICAN TOURISTS are referred to the Hotel Register, Harper's Guide, &c. LIVERY AND POSTING ESTABLISHMENT. Under the patronage of H.R.H. the Prince of Wales.　　**J. PENROSE, Proprietor.**

HARKER'S YORK HOTEL,
ST. HELEN'S SQUARE,
YORK.

This long-established and first-class Family Hotel is in the best situation in the City, being nearest to the Minster, the Ruins of St. Mary's Abbey, &c., &c.; and within five minutes' walk of the Railway Station.

This Hotel is largely patronised by American Visitors.

P. MATTHEWS, Proprietor.

An advertisement for the Black Swan, 1873.

Striving desperately to revive the good old days of quadrille and minuet, they organised, in 1835, an October meeting which managed to brush away many of the cobwebs. The band of the 10th Hussars provided the music, to which more than eight hundred danced, but, somehow, something was missing. Dancing just wasn't the answer.

The same year saw the introduction at York of a new race, The Champagne Stakes – yet another convivial encounter, the victor of which had to contribute two dozen bottles of champagne to the Hunt Club. The race fizzled out after two years, but it was to reappear in much more telling form during the next decade.

Meanwhile, just who was organising things at Knavesmire? Hunt Club members were also members of the Gimcrack Club, which was still, merrily and rosily, holding its superb annual dinners. And among the Gimcrack Club members were the Race Committee.

But who was going to DO something about York races?

11

John Orton's Loyalty Betrayed
The tragedy behind the revival

 Good, hard working, ever faithful John Orton was sitting in a large, packed room at Lockwood's Hotel in York. The date was November 17, 1842, and, for once, all eyes were upon him. Race judge at Knavesmire for the past twelve years, he had been factotum to the Race Committee for far longer. Now they were appointing him clerk of the course, with the request that he should perform the minor miracle of putting York races back on their feet.

Orton glanced round at the subscribers who fully expected that their subscriptions would help work the necessary magic. His glance also took in seventeen men, headed by Mr William North, who had been chosen to supervise both the racing fund and the way in which the races were to be run and organised. It sounded perilously like a real Race Committee. So it was, but Orton was soon to learn how little it appreciated his devotion.

The racing fund – we might call it an emergency fund – had been opened at an earlier meeting that year, when everyone came out with the now-familiar lament about the decline and fall of York, 'notwithstanding that the city has the advantage of a racecourse equal, if not superior, to any in the kingdom.' This observation compared favourably with that of a visitor, who obviously liked a little quality in his racing: 'A more miserable affair than York August meeting it has never been my misfortune to attend – everything reached the climax of dullness. No company, bad sport and no betting.' The only thing in York's favour was that its plight couldn't be any worse.

Orton was more than willing to oblige, but there was one big problem – Lord George Bentinck, sportsman and third son of the Duke of Portland. Bentinck, a relentless, domineering personality, both in politics and on the Turf, had, for some reason, developed an obsessive hatred for Orton.

This, in itself, was bearable, but the constant nightmare for Orton was that Lord George, who made plain his liking for Doncaster, indulged in moral blackmail, informing the Race Committee that he would never be seen at York while Orton had any connections with the meetings there.

But the most deplorable feature of the whole affair was that the Race Committee succumbed to the pressure, sacrificing principle for expediency – the sad result of allowing politics, of whatever shade, to influence sport.

In the three remaining years before his fall from grace, however, John

Lord George Bentinck.

93

Orton helped the Race Committee introduce sweeping changes at Knavesmire. More money was coming in, and the city of York itself was aware that it should be digging into its pockets.

Orton had already preached the basic message that you get what you pay for: 'The City of York should not be satisfied with dealing us out such short measure, for, as all men like the most they can get for their money, if they persevere in dealing out such meagre bills of fare, I fear they will have few visitors.'

This doctrine can, however, lead to a generous subscriber seeking ownership. Doncaster was already run by the corporation there, and several take-over bids were to be made by York's City Council. Only skilful diplomacy was to save York going the same way as Doncaster.

At this time, however, York had good reason to cringe whenever Doncaster's Town Moor was mentioned. For while York, originally the proudest racecourse in the land, had degenerated into a sort of Turfing playground, Doncaster had got to work, resulting in the resounding success of the St Leger.

But self-recrimination had to end at Knavesmire, and Orton got down to work. The result, in 1843, was The Great Ebor Handicap, later to be known, simply, as The Ebor. It was, somehow, fitting, that York's first great race should bear the Roman name for the city, Eboracum having been the birthplace of racing in this country. Pagan, ridden by Sim Templeman, was the first winner of this event, with a Colonel Cradock the proud owner. The race was over two miles and the Race Committee added two hundred pounds to the stakes.

Fresh air was at last blowing across Knavesmire, The Great Ebor spearheading sweeping changes two years later. Excitement was contagious as down came all the wooden buildings, to be replaced by brick ones. That horse-shoe track became circular, cutting out the distant bulge by Middlethorpe village. There was a pretty lawn in front of the grandstand, and much of the course was railed in. The Great Ebor was modified to one and three-quarter miles, and a five-furlong sprint course appeared.

But Orton was still hounded by the hatred of Lord George Bentinck who, as a Parliamentarian, could advocate compassion for the Irish in their economic plight and call for the acknowledgement of religious liberty. Had he practised tolerance nearer home, such a quality would have been better appreciated.

He refused to take the knife out of Orton's back, and the Clerk of Course was dismissed, on some trumped-up excuse. Orton already owned the Turf Coffee House in York, where he prided himself on his wines. He also took bets there. But when he sought solace in the coffee house after his dismissal, it merely spelled his speedy doom. Orton took to the bottle, drinking himself to death with his own liquor within weeks of his having helped with the latest improvements.

A certain fondness for Orton, a great racing recorder, still prevails. Just

The work-box made from part of the old winning-post.

after the first Great Ebor was run, the old oak winning-post was taken down. Part of it was made into a work-box, which Orton gave to his daughter. On it were inscribed these words: 'Part of the old winning-post at York, taken down in 1843, to which, for upwards of half a century, hundreds of the first horses on the British Turf struggled for glory and renown, in the days when genuine purity, sterling honesty and true nobility adorned the national pastime – John Orton, judge.'

Bentinck, whose life was studded with racing successes, gained a reputation for fighting against dishonest practices on the Turf. He died, three years after Orton, while walking near Welbeck Abbey. He was forty-six.

The fall of John Orton showed clearly that the Gimcrack Club members of his day were not depicted on that chunk of oak. Despite the improvements, brought about by harsh economic reality, York would not gain the style and standards to which it was entitled until much later.

In the meantime, who was to help carry on the task undertaken by Orton? The man to take up the baton was one of the stewards at York – Mr R M Jaques, who hadn't forgotten that little horse Gimcrack if everyone else had. What more appropriate than that the great little horse, that inspired those early men at York, should lend its name to a quality race there.

So, in 1846, was born the Gimcrack Stakes – a race which was to gain national fame, though little did anyone so imagine at the time. Jaques had

A flask presented to John Orton and now in the Racing Museum, York.

been encouraged by the old members of the Yorkshire Union Hunt Club, who had organised the short-lived Champagne Stakes. The club had folded, and its members became Gimcracks, joining in the hearty annual dinners in the heavily-beamed Punch Bowl Inn.

Gimcrack gave the title sparkle, and the longer-serving Gimcrack Club members had no objection to the sparkle of champagne being retained. The owner of the winning horse had, therefore, to give three dozen bottles of champagne to the Gimcrack Club. He would, naturally, be invited to the annual feast in the Punch Bowl, where he would be called upon to make a speech.

This first speech was a memorable one, even though we haven't the faintest idea what Admiral Harcourt of Masham said. For the winning owner's speech at the Gimcrack dinner was to become an event to which the racing world would attach the utmost importance – an annual milestone in Turfing oration, being both critical and progressive.

The race was for two-year-old colts, to carry eight stone and seven pounds, and fillies, to carry eight stone and two pounds, with the winner of the Prince of Wales Stakes to carry an extra three pounds. The admiral's winning horse was a bay filly, Ellerdale, ridden by the Middleham jockey, Tommy Lye and trained at Middleham by Tom Dawson – an entirely Yorkshire victory.

It was poetic justice that the man who was chiefly responsible for the Gimcrack Stakes, then run over a mile, should be called upon to make the winning owner's speech after his triumph in the fourth running of the race. Mildew, with that fine jockey Nat Flatman up, obliged for Mr Jaques.

So little Gimcrack had gained immortality both in spirit and on the Turf, through a race which was to feature some of the great horses of all time. The William I'Anson-trained Blink Bonny, subsequently to win both Derby and Oaks, was the first of the 'greats' to snatch the prize, beating Lord Zetland's Skirmisher by two lengths in 1856.

Names such as Bahram and Gulf Stream were to feature in the roll-call of winners much later, but the magic of the Gimcrack Stakes – cut to a straight six furlongs just before the dawn of the twentieth century – still emanates from the ghost of that gutsy little grey horse.

The Ebor Handicap, despite lacking the Gimcrack's touch of romance, radiated its own, unique warmth. Ebor Day at York was to become a great place of assembly for the working muscle of the country – shipbuilders from Clydebank, steelworkers and miners from Durham and Yorkshire, textile workers from the Lancashire mills. Many a cloth cap became airborne when that popular combination of Brown Jack and Steve Donoghue was first past the post in 1931.

Gimcrack Day featured different shades of colour between the two world wars, when fashion dominated the event, probably far more than it should have done. When Princess Mary witnessed Town Guard's victory in 1922, the county and members' stands were buzzing with activity, in marked contrast to the popular enclosures, where inertia was extremely evident. Bert

97

Higgins had decided that this was not his scene. But the entire August meeting is now so rich that our Bert doesn't know which day to pick, his best choice being all three.

At about the time that both the Gimcrack and the Great Ebor were introduced, York Race Committee decided to clamp down on cheats and on racing's defaulters. Horses were being substituted at the last moment; there were false ages, false names and, last but not least, false people.

New regulations began to bite when the stewards announced that no horse would be allowed to compete for any stake at York unless its mouth had been examined by a veterinary surgeon.

Anyone who had defaulted on stakes, forfeits or bets was refused entrance to the grandstand, and those who managed to dodge through were shown the way out as soon as they were spotted. No-one was allowed to enter a race, or enter a horse of which he was the owner, if he had welshed on a bet.

But York races, as we have seen, came in for their fair share of criticism, and the critics maintained their moans, many of them justified, throughout much of the eighteenth century. One critic was particularly outspoken – Admiral Rous, who gained the title of 'Turf Dictator'.

'Rous the Grouse' continually harped on about the meanness of York Race Committee, in an age when deductions from prize money were common. So much went towards the judge, and so much towards 'expenses'. The man who was directly in the firing line, and who possibly held the record for the number of roustings received from Rous, was a clerk of the course, Mr Richard Johnson.

The admiral also aired his views publicly: 'At York, where they have illegally received, in two years, two thousand, one hundred and thirty-eight pounds for sales by auction, they cannot afford to give a miserable fifty pound place without a demand of five pounds from the winner besides the entrance money.'

But Admiral Rous undoubtedly meant well, and bore a grudging admiration for York races. The year in which he levelled his criticisms was 1866, and some fifteen years previously, when he bore the rank of captain, he had the distinction of handicapping the last of the great challenge matches – a match which will live for ever.

The place was Knavesmire, and the protagonists Voltigeur and The Flying Dutchman. Those who witnessed the event were to recount it with pride to their children and grand-children. Among them was a twenty-two-year-old man, who became a member of York Race Committee only a year after that public rousting from the admiral.

The young man, whose greatcoat buttonhole invariably sported rose or carnation, had plenty of time in which to bring that great race back to life. The tale of the battle of the giants would entertain his great-grandchildren . . . when they were adult! For the man with the flower in his buttonhole last captivated his audience in 1929, when he was one hundred years old. And this is what grand old Mr James Melrose told them . . .

98

Admiral Rous and George Payne.

12

The Great Match of 1851
Voltigeur v The Flying Dutchman

 Thomas Dundas, Earl of Zetland, took a long, hard look at the yearling which was being paraded before him. A less likely prospect he hadn't clapped eyes on for a long time.

'Are you serious?' he asked the man standing at his side.

'I've never been more serious in my life Your Lordship', replied the earl's trainer, Robert Hill. 'I advise you to buy him.'

'Where is he from?'

'Out of Martha Lynn by Voltaire. Bred by Robert Stephenson at Hartlepool. It'll be a good 'un.'

That was hardly likely, thought Lord Zetland. In any case, he wasn't in the mood for just another 'good 'un', he was looking for a great one. Now in his fifties, he still hadn't owned a Derby winner – his great ambition. And prospects seemed to grow dimmer every year.

He cast a glance around the other owners, who were deep in conversation, and who had anything on their minds except the yearling which was ambling before them. Wouldn't it be fine to snatch a prize prospect from under their noses? But this wasn't the one.

'No, definitely not,' said Lord Zetland. And that was that ... for the time being.

Hill was distinctly disappointed, but he didn't argue the point. When the boss made up his mind that was that. But so often Lord Zetland made rash decisions which he later regretted. Was this another one? The second Earl of Zetland had a reputation for honesty, but he was also known to be of 'somewhat impulsive disposition'.

The following spring, Lord Zetland was relaxing at his home – Aske Hall near Richmond – and pondering over the decision he had made at those yearling sales. His mind also wandered towards the good old Black Swan in York, and towards Knavesmire.

Knavesmire and Aske Hall – there was a connection of which he was well aware. Robert Aske, a member of the family whose name the hall bore, had led that Pilgrimage of Grace against Henry VIII – an uprising which was quelled by the Knavesmire gallows. Aske's body finished in Clifford's Tower, hanging in chains.

But Lord Zetland's thoughts kept wandering back to that yearling. Should

Voltigeur with Lady Zetland from a contemporary photography.

he change his mind? Should he take a chance on Hill's intuition? He was definitely open to a little extra persuasion.

'You look miles away, Charles.'

Here was a sympathetic ear – his brother-in-law and perpetual adviser, Robert Williamson.

'Yes, as a matter of fact I was. Look here, I want your advice.'

'Before you go on, I've got some advice for you. Buy that yearling, you can get him for a thousand guineas.'

Archibald William Montgomery, the thirteenth Earl of Eglinton, was a charming, likeable fellow, who was not averse to a bit of flattery and who had a popular habit of throwing his money around. He was particularly welcome among those who happened to be within catching distance.

This year of 1849 was a vintage one, both for Lord Eglinton and for the expert fieldsmen who tagged on behind him. For his prize possession, a colt called Flying Dutchman, had won both the Derby and the St Leger. And that was something that his old rival, Zetland, couldn't match.

There was a lot of talk about this Voltigeur, which Hill was training up at Zetland's place near Richmond. They were trying it in next year's Derby, and everybody in Yorkshire seemed to be losing his senses over the colt as the days shortened into winter. But, whatever it did, Voltigeur would never be the equal of the Dutchman. Voltigeur was Yorkshire bred and Yorkshire trained was it? So was The Flying Dutchman. Zetland couldn't beat Eglinton on that score either! In one sense it was a pity that the Dutchman had already run his Derby. Eglinton would have relished a personal victory over Zetland in the major classic.

Feelings were far different on Lord Zetland's estates, and the Voltigeur betting fever which broke out there spread throughout the county. The earl, Lord Lieutenant of the North Riding, was eating, drinking and sleeping Voltigeur. Every tenant on his lands, every servant in the hall, was putting his or her last penny, and more, on it.

Came the spring of 1850, and good Yorkshire money was still cascading onto Voltigeur's shoulders. And the odds were tempting, with the so-called pundits in the south causing a price of about 20–1.

Lord Zetland was jovially disposed as he came down to breakfast one bright morning, but his complexion became ominously cloudy when he opened the mail. The clouds then burst as he thundered: 'Never! Pay a four hundred pound forfeit on Voltigeur? Never!' But the letter made it clear that, if the forfeit due were not paid, Voltigeur couldn't start in the Derby.

'Voltigeur is to be scratched', announced Lord Zetland to his trainer Hill. Scratched! The news buzzed around the estates like a busy bee among the clover. Servants were stunned, farm-hands frantic and maids amazed. All that betting, all that excitement, all that commitment.

Dismay soon turned to desperation as the tenants realised how costly their 'cert' was going to prove for them. To whom could they turn? There was only one answer – Robert Williamson. The tenants put their dire position to his ever-sympathetic ear.

Lord Zetland was sitting quietly, studying his feet, and wondering if he'd been a little rash. The forfeit really should be paid. And he would let down a lot of people if he pulled out Voltigeur. He'd always longed for a Derby winner, and here he was, throwing away the chance of a lifetime. He needed someone to talk him into making the necessary decision.

Intuitively, Robert entered the room when his guidance was most needed. 'I've just had a deputation from the tenants. If Voltigeur is scratched they will be in a desperate situation. They've put every spare penny on it. Pay the forfeit and let Voltigeur run.'

Lord Zetland's coachman, already a mountain of mufflers and coat-flaps, felt even bigger as he went to collect his Derby winnings. Voltigeur had come in at 16–1, so that meant he was collecting two hundred pounds! He was rich, incredibly, gloriously rich. Everyone on the estate was appreciably better off, but none so affluent as that coachman.

The Flying Dutchman.

Voltigeur was flying high. The inimitable Yorkshire combination of himself, Lord Zetland and Robert Hill went on to take the St Leger, but it was in the Doncaster Gold Cup, run only two days after the Leger, that the first clash of the Titans – The Flying Dutchman and Voltigeur – took place. At last Lord Eglinton could show the true worth of the 'unbeatable' Dutchman.

Nat Flatman was on Voltigeur, the pair nudging in two lengths behind the Dutchman for much of the running. Then it happened. The Flying Dutchman suddenly dried up, leaving a delirious crowd to cheer in Voltigeur, while Eglinton, shocked and pale, leaned against the wall of the Jockey Club stand for support.

Lord Zetland was triumphant. Within one year he had realised three ambitions – to win the Derby, to take the St Leger and to beat Eglinton's Dutchman. But the matter couldn't rest here.

'We must have a return,' said Lord Eglinton to his rival.

'Naturally,' said Lord Zetland. 'A straight match on the best course in the country – York. Shall we say over two miles for a thousand pounds?'

'You're on.'

The 'Mucky Duck' in York had never done such a roaring trade as in that

May of 1851. There was Rous the Grouse, Glasgow the Volcano, 'Owd Sir Tatton, His Royal Highness Prince Henry of the Netherlands ('' 'is English was that good 'e 'ad to be a foreigner'), Duke and Duchess of Roxburghe, Duke of Leeds, Earl of Scarborough, Earl of Chesterfield, Lord and Lady Bolton and, of course, the Earl and Countess of Zetland and the Earl and Countess of Eglinton.

At the George Inn across the road you couldn't hear yourself speak. They'd walked in from all over the place, and many hadn't had a square meal for a couple of days. A lot of people had come by train, and they all seemed to think a bed could be made to appear from thin air. The floors were full, as were the hedges outside town.

When the cock crew to welcome the dawn of May 13 men shuffled to their feet by the thousand, shivering from the damp that had crept under the clothes, under their skin, while they slept. Circulation was rubbed back into stiff shoulders and necks, hands were blown warm and vitality stamped back into numbed feet. The great trek to Knavesmire was under way.

Trainloads were still rumbling into York as the army of early-birds converged on Knavesmire. The walking multitudes were unaware of their weariness, their excitement forming a natural antidote. Many had trudged fifty miles or more, and would appreciate their fatigue only when they had completed the return journey. Thousands who could spare neither the time nor the money were still determined to witness the great match.

Miners and hardware workers from South Yorkshire, factory hands from Leeds, farmers and farm-hands from throughout the north, joined the curious from the south, ensuring a place near the rails well before the race. Special trains had been packed four hours before their departure.

Captain Rous, as he then was, had already settled the handicap problem, giving The Flying Dutchman eight stone, eight-and-a-half pounds and Voltigeur eight stone.

The world of racing held its breath as the great champions went to the line together. Nat Flatman was on Voltigeur again, with C. Marlow on the Dutchman. 'They're off!' A gigantic roar swelled through the air as the famous rivals launched themselves into the great decider.

Flatman decided on fast running from the start, pulling three lengths clear of The Flying Dutchman at top speed. But, as they rounded the final bend, Marlow turned on the pressure. They passed the stands stride for stride, the crowd at fever pitch. But this time it was the younger Voltigeur who faded first, the Dutchman gained the verdict.

So Lord Eglinton had gained his revenge. But, in one sense, he and Lord Zetland settled for a draw. Eglington was magnanimous in victory, and Zetland acknowledged the ultimate defeat. 'But', he told Eglinton over drinks, 'you will always remember the only horse to beat your Dutchman – Voltigeur.'

Before the great race Lord Eglinton had committed The Flying Dutchman to go into stud with a new breeding company on Knavesmire. The Dutchman

Flying Dutchman wins from Voltigeur at York.

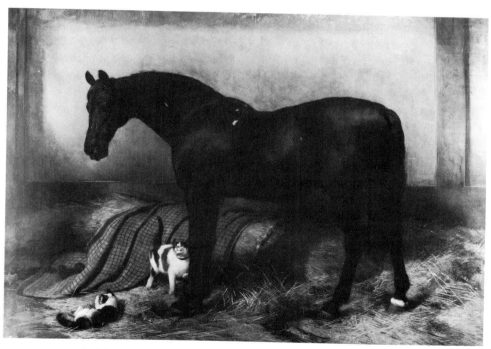

Voltigeur and friends, from the painting by Sir Edwin Landseer.

was their first purchase, and one of great prestige, provided he wasn't beaten by Voltigeur. The company, facing the real possibility of another defeat for the Dutchman, persuaded Eglinton to hang onto the colt until after the Knavesmire verdict.

As for Voltigeur, his great days were almost over. But one little pal stuck by, or rather on, him, win or lose – an old cat which wandered round the stables near Richmond. The cat's favourite sleeping place was on Voltigeur's back, day in, day out. And when Voltigeur closed his eyes at night the cat went on the prowl. But, like most cats, it had a broad streak of selfishness, and would 'go nap' on Voltigeur only if the covers were on the horse. A bare-back bed was not to his liking.

Voltigeur did have one more victory to come, the following year at York. Rather ironically, he won The Flying Dutchman Handicap.

This was his last race before he was retired to stud. In 1874 he was badly kicked by a mare, and died soon afterwards.

But the great rivalry between Voltigeur and The Flying Dutchman had a happy sequel. Voltigeur's son, Vedette, was mated with The Flying Duchess, daughter of The Flying Dutchman. And it was their offspring, Galopin, which won the Derby of 1875.

Was it not fitting that the memory of such a great horse should be kept alive? This was not to happen until nearly a century later – at the dawn of the golden age at York. In 1950 The Voltigeur Stakes was inaugurated, blossoming into The Great Voltigeur Stakes seven years later.

The centre-piece of a dinner service presented to the winner of the 1982 Great Voltigeur Stakes.

13

James Melrose

James Melrose bustled around the house, sprucing himself up before making the usual mile-long Sunday morning walk to attend matins at York Minster.

Diamond-headed tie-pin; cuffs in order; spats straight; shoes shining; pick up the cane; last check on the top hat. Wait a minute, something missing – the buttonhole flower. An orchid would be a change this fine morning, after three carnation days on the trot.

'Morning Mrs Melrose, Mr Melrose. Morning children. Congratulations Mr Melrose, I hear you're on the Race Committee.'

Indeed he was. James Melrose wasn't forty years old yet, and this was the biggest honour that he had received. The year was 1867, and only a few years previously Melrose had carried out a task which undoubtedly led to his being invited to join the committee.

Melrose and Hornsey, surveyors and land agents, had been called in to fight the morass into which much of Knavesmire was again deteriorating. The aftermath of a wet spell could still cause a horse to disappear up to its knees if it hit a bad patch on the course. James Melrose was responsible for the drainage – a job well done. He'd always been interested in Knavesmire though, ever since he watched that Voltigeur and Flying Dutchman match.

'Morning Mrs Melrose, Mr Melrose. Morning children. Had any good bets recently Mr Melrose?'

'I never bet dear fellow', called out Melrose, maintaining the domestic walking pace. 'Last wager I had was on Voltigeur when it won the St Leger in 1850. It was a local bookmaker. Couldn't pay out, so I told him to take his time. Then I took to thinking. If I became too keen on the money side of racing I might put myself in a position of liability. So I swore I wouldn't bet again.'

He chuckled as he remembered that other bookmaker at York – the one who offered ludicrous odds to a man with more money than sense. He asked the bookie why he was being so extravagant. Lowering his voice confidentially, the sly old fox replied: 'Scratched this morning Mr James, scratched this morning.'

Melrose the Rose was right on time at every pausing point, timing the family's arrival at York Minster neither too early nor too late.

James Melrose (left) *aged 17, and aged 47.*

'Morning Mrs Melrose, Mr Melrose. Morning children.' A woman's voice came down from a first-floor window. 'I was just telling my husband, you always know exactly what time it is when Mr Melrose passes by on a Sunday morning.'

Another face appeared at the window – her husband's. 'Mr Melrose, I've got a bit of a problem that you might be able to help me with. My wall fruit's riddled with disease.'

'Point your walls', called out Melrose, by now exactly ten yards past the house.

'Why point the walls Mr Melrose?'

'If you don't they'll decay. The lime falls out and insects lay their eggs in the cracks in winter. That means that the fruit will be destroyed when the warm weather comes. It's a tip that I was given.'

Through Bootham Bar, down Petergate, and there, suddenly, loomed the massive western towers of York Minister, the elaborate traceries of their huge windows presenting a maze of stone, studded with splashes of glazed colour.

In through the door, right on time, and down the knave, beneath towering vaults which formed a man-made celestial dome. Footsteps echoed on towards the choir, past the transept with its simple, elegant lances of early-English glass.

The service began, and as the organ of this great church, the largest gothic cathedral in Europe, bellowed out triumphantly, Mr Melrose found his mind wandering to racing, to Knavesmire, then back to the Minster, before returning to racing.

Monarchs had been wed here; monarchs had been crowned here. The history of England was all here, going back to the laying of those first foundations, more than twelve hundred years previously.

Here was buried Lord Rockingham, the man who first put York races on their feet. And that reminded Melrose of the grandstand. The new county stand was another step forward. Some of the behaviour in the stands had been leaving a lot to be desired. The county stand would help improve social standards. No-one wanted affairs to slip back to the standards of the bad old days.

The choir sang lightly, harmoniously on, the silvery notes of the boy sopranos coming from on high. 'Run the good race', somebody said. Little did James Melrose realise that his personal race would last a century. One thing he did realise though, was that racing at York could still be improved.

National Hunt racing had started at Knavesmire, but James Melrose thought it wouldn't last. Did they want quality flat racing or not? Look at that Great Yorkshire Handicap they'd had this year, with all its stupid entry stipulations: 'Horses must have been hunted regularly with the York and Ainsty and Bramham Moor Hounds, and belong to farmers occupying lands, and to tradesmen carrying on their business in either of the above hunts, and

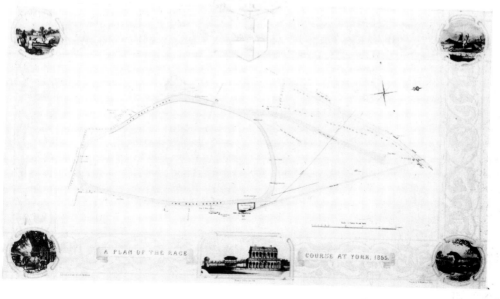

A PLAN OF THE RACE COURSE AT YORK, 1855.

be ridden by farmers and tradesmen so qualified, or their sons.' What sort of nonsense was this? Knavesmire was a top course. There were however certain concessions: 'gentlemen residing in Yorkshire, or officers in the Army or Navy allowed to ride.' That threw the doors wide open! What a way to draw the crowds! What a way to attract the miners! Had they heard of a little thing called the Industrial Revolution? York was in grave danger of resting on the laurels of the Ebor Handicap and Gimcrack Stakes. To stand still was to move backwards.

The organ thumped out its finale, and the congregation shuffled into the aisles. 'A lovely service dear', said his wife. 'Yes', replied Melrose, 'it certainly gave plenty of food for thought.'

14

Frederick Vyner
Heroic death of a great supporter

 The spring meeting of 1870 was the quietest and saddest that Knavesmire had ever known. Society had shunned the meeting as a mark of respect to a young man who had been murdered in a distant land.

Frederick Grantham Vyner, a regular attender at York races, had decided against going to the spring meeting that year. Frederick, who was only twenty-three, and who had been fighting ill health for most of his existence, was persuaded that a change might do him good, particularly in the warm, gentle air of Greece.

The youngest son of Lady Mary Vyner, of Newby Hall, near Ripon, Yorkshire, he desperately wanted to prove that he could mix with the other fellows when they hunted or went racing, despite his weakness.

He deeply regretted not being able to go to York that year, particularly as he always seemed to be so jolly popular there. He couldn't understand why everybody seemed to like him. He wasn't particularly good at anything, and he could never think up any good jokes. He was just himself.

Just recently his health had appeared to be picking up a little, and Lord Muncaster said this was all the more reason why he should go with him and his party to Marathon in Greece to wander round the ancient battlefield.

His travelling companions were Lord and Lady Muncaster, Mr Herbert, who was the secretary to the British Legation in Athens, Mr Edward Lloyd, a barrister, who was accompanied by his wife and small daughter and Count Alberto de Boyl.

They made their way to Marathon with a police escort – a basic precaution as the route was notorious for bandits. But the carriage seemed safe enough. They had a splendid day at the battlefield. And Frederick particularly appreciated the splendid picnic. The way back seemed peaceful enough, and he couldn't understand why the policemen were so nervous. The two up front appeared particularly edgy.

Like most terrible incidents it happened without any distinct warning. There was a cracking sound, and those policemen weren't on their horses any more. The air was full of dust and screaming and shouting, and he couldn't understand a single word. The other policemen had their arms in the air, and there were some other grimy-looking people on horseback. They were Greek and they must have come from behind bushes. They each held a carbine as though it was the extension of an arm, and they were all festooned with bandoliers.

One of the policemen leaned into the carriage, his face drained of expression, and gabbled something in Greek. 'They want us to get out', said Mr Herbert.

As they lined up under the mellowing sun the little girl, shaking with terror, buried herself in her mother's skirts. One of the bandits, who seemed to be in charge, shouted something and pointed to the nearby mountains.

'They're taking us into the hills', announced Mr Herbert.

The two dead policemen were dragged into the bushes, and one of the bandits took charge of the carriage and pair, heading them towards some obscure and undetectable spot.

Spare horses seemed to be everywhere, as the stunned group were told to mount. The screaming child was swung from her mother's arms onto the back of a bandit's horse and the women were told to sit behind their husbands and hold on tight. Each horse received a crack on the flanks as the yelling bandits stampeded the group towards the hills, the child's screams muffled by the thunder of hooves.

Frederick Vyner couldn't relate what was happening to reality. He'd rarely been outside Yorkshire and here he was, on his first trip abroad, galloping into some nightmare. The pace was making him feel sick, and, when he managed to catch some breath, he started coughing.

The group neared some hillocks, and the pace slowed to a canter. The canter became a trot as the bandits' leader gesticulated towards what proved to be a small hidden valley.

Suddenly everything was still, the uneasy silence punctuated only by Frederick's heavy bouts of coughing. The bandits' leader ambled up and down, triumphantly scrutinising each of his prisoners. He shouted something to Mr Herbert.

'Everyone dismount,' said the legation secretary, his face ashen. The little girl scampered to her mother as the dazed party formed a line.

'I know who this man is,' Mr Herbert told them quietly. 'They call him Takos, and he can be ruthless. Do what he says and do not provoke him.'

'My God, what about the ladies?' muttered Lord Muncaster.

'Don't worry, these men have certain rules. They don't molest women. They're after money, but they'll kill for it if they have to.'

Takos and one of his lieutenants confronted each victim in turn, pointing to pockets, to wrists, to necks, to ears. Money, valuables, papers, passed from pale hands into swarthy, hardened ones.

The policemen who had survived the ambush were allowed to sit on some nearby rocks, one of the bandits guarding them.

Takos crammed the money and valuables into a bag which was hanging from his saddle, but retained some of the papers that he had taken from the men.

Frederick started coughing again. One of the bandits made a remark about him, and they all burst out laughing. Well, at least he'd caused some amusement.

Takos drew his lieutenant to one side, and they both examined the papers. Suddenly Takos placed a hand on his companion's arm, and drew his attention to a particular letter which Mr Herbert had received from the Greek Government.

There was a pause, before the pair gazed at one another in a mutual expression of amazement. The amazement turned to yells of triumph. They slapped their knees, punched each other in the chest and leaped into the air.

Takos called Mr Herbert over, and held him in deep conversation, prodding the Englishman's shoulder at regular intervals, as though driving home a point. Herbert approached the group with grave deliberation.

'I'm afraid that Takos has found out who we are. I'm awfully sorry about this, but they've taken a letter which was written to me in Greek. It was about the visit. We're all named.'

'Good heavens man! That surely will convince the blackguard that he's gone too far,' exclaimed Lord Muncaster. 'In any case, he has all the money we possess.'

'You're missing the point', said Mr Herbert, who was far nearer the world of reality than Muncaster. 'He does know what we possess, and he wants quite a slice of it. To be more precise he wants fifty thousand pounds.'

Lord Muncaster laughed scornfully: 'Well he jolly well can't have it.'

Mr Herbert replied slowly, earnestly and emphatically: 'I must tell you what Takos is going to do. He is releasing the ladies and the child, but he is holding the rest of us as hostages. All, that is, except one of us, preferably yourself, Lord Muncaster, or you Mr Vyner. The reason for this is that he needs someone to raise the ransom money. They'll allow the policemen to escort the ladies back to Athens, and their men will give cover in case any other bandits attempt to molest the party.'

'And what happens if something goes wrong?' asked a now shaken Lord Muncaster.

'Takos will kill all four of us.'

The shock made Frederick stop coughing. Suddenly, he found himself saying words that seemed to be coming from someone else.

'Lord Muncaster must go. I am of little consequence. In any case I am certain that the matter will be resolved satisfactorily if Lord Muncaster handles the negotiations.'

Muncaster protested. Vyner had come at his, Muncaster's, invitation and he felt personally responsible for the safety of the young man, whose health the trip had been intended to improve, not impair. But Frederick would have none of it. So Muncaster decided to take a gamble.

'We'll toss for it.'

'What do we use for a coin?'

Herbert had the answer to that dilemma. Walking over to Takos he held out his hand and asked the bandit chief if he could lend him an English coin. Takos burst into laughter, went over to the saddlebag, took out a coin, gave it to Mr Herbert and said a few quiet words to him.

Returning to the group, Herbert handed the vital coin to Muncaster. 'Takos says that the coin is to be returned to him. He will pierce a hole in it and hang it around his neck as a special memento.'

'Shall you call, Freddie, or shall I?' asked Muncaster.

'It doesn't matter.'

'Right, I'll toss up and you call.'

The bandits watched the proceedings with expressions varying from amazement to bewilderment. The English, undoubtedly, were mad.

The coin sang into the warm air.

'Heads,' called Vyner. Heads it was.

'Well, that settles it,' said Muncaster.

'Yes, it does. You go, I stay.'

Muncaster protested. Vyner had won the toss, so Vyner must return to Athens with the ladies.

Frederick shook his head. 'I won the toss, so I have the choice. That is my right. If a fellow wins the toss at cricket he can put the opposition in to bat, or he can choose to bat himself. In any case you simply said "We'll toss for it." You didn't specify what. If something happens to me it is of little consequence. My health seems unlikely to improve; in fact I am feeling positively ill. Whether I can survive for a few more years I know not, but at least I can be of some use now. And remember, you have Lady Muncaster to think of.'

Muncaster fought hard to reconcile himself to the decision which he realised he must make. A glance at the inflexible Vyner, and another at the tearful Lady Muncaster, put the issue beyond doubt.

As the party took its leave, the four men stood in painful silence. Edward Lloyd would not be seeing his wife and daughter again.

Now began the ten never-ending days of anxiety. Takos, who adopted the principle that it is difficult to hit a moving target, dragged Frederick and his companions from place to place every night, allowing them to rest, their clothing sodden, only during the daytime.

Frederick found it increasingly difficult to breathe properly, and the continual physical effort, coupled with the poor food and conditions, sapped his energy almost to the point of total exhaustion.

Meanwhile Lord Muncaster had to deal with an equally trigger-happy Greek Government, whose first inclination was to send out the troops.

'I beg you not to send out the army to look for Takos,' said Muncaster to the minister responsible. 'For he will have no hesitation in killing my friends.' The minister was about to reply when an official came into the room and handed him a note. His expression became fixed as he read it.

'Lord Muncaster, I gather that you have already been able to guarantee raising the ransom money. I can now tell you that Takos has sent word that he has lowered the amount to twenty-five thousand pounds.'

'That is good news,' replied Muncaster. 'It surely means that he is weakening. Any hasty action on our part would serve no purpose.'

'It is not as simple as that Lord Muncaster,' replied the minister. 'Takos seeks the guarantee of an amnesty.'

'Is that a problem?'

'It most certainly is. It is against the constitution of the Greek Government to grant amnesties to criminals. We have been after Takos for some time, and you have no assurance that he will not kill your friends even if he receives the money.'

Muncaster had hit a brick wall, and he knew it. The Greeks would not bargain with terrorists. As the negotiations dragged on, the Greek Government became edgy. Meanwhile, in the hills, the condition of the captives was itself a cause for concern.

The situation became explosive, and the Greeks, frustrated and angry, sent the cavalry out into the mountains to surround Takos and his band. Not wishing to be attacked themselves, they chose the high ground, hoping that their appearance would flush Takos out.

As they scoured the ravines below they spotted the bandits and their captives. The soldiers, reacting instinctively, and not seeking tactical instructions, let loose a volley of rifle fire.

The shots were wide and wild, but they spelled the end for the hostages.

There was pandemonium in the ravine as Takos screamed to his men to take cover and bring the captives with them. Screened by boulders and trees, he wheeled round to face the doomed quartet, his face contorted with rage.

Pointing to Mr Herbert and Mr Lloyd he screeched out a command. A rain of bullets poured through the two men, hurling them from their horses. As they lay squirming on the ground the hail of fire continued, knocking the bodies from side to side.

When there was little left to distinguish, and when rage had burned itself out, Takos pointed down the ravine to the open plain, the only possible escape route. Takos headed the gallop for freedom, with Frederick Vyner and Count Alberto, shocked, exhausted and weak from the tension, the only remaining cards that he had to deal.

Frederick was in a weird trance. His spirit seemed to have left his body, as they thundered across the plain, it was as though he were looking down on himself from on high.

Suddenly Takos wheeled the party to a halt. He had realised that any hopes of an amnesty were dashed. He was also aware that not a pound, not a drachma, of ransom money would come his way.

He barked an order to his men, who raised their rifles. Frederick looked down from the heavens as the bullets cut Count Alberto and himself down.

At last he would stop that infernal coughing.

The strident chords from the organ of York Minster warmed the heart and cheered the spirit as the congregation filtered quietly from the choir at the close of matins.

'A pleasant service dear,' said Mrs Melrose to her husband, who had chosen a pink carnation for that particular Sunday in January 1890.

'Yes, it certainly gave more food for thought,' replied James Melrose, as he looked reflectively along the south wall. He was now sixty-two and, apart from having been Lord Mayor of York, he was chairman of the Race Committee, a position he had held for fifteen years.

'I was just thinking how much things have improved since we had a special committee to keep an eye on the conduct in the county stand. But it's such a pity that the standards of many people who are involved in racing at Knavesmire still leave a lot to be desired.'

His wife paused at a memorial on the wall which seemed to carry some sort of message. 'Can you make out what it says James?' she asked. 'My eyesight isn't quite what it used to be.'

'Yes, that's the one they put up for Frederick Vyner,' Melrose replied. 'Can't you remember? I was here when it was unveiled. Splendid fellow he was. His mother raised that ransom, you know, and when he was murdered she decided to use the money to have a church built at Skelton, on the Newby Estate, in his memory.'

'Yes dear, but would you mind telling me what it says.'

'It says, "In memory of Frederick Vyner, aged twenty-three, who was taken prisoner by Greek brigands in the neighbourhood of Athens, April 11, 1870, and murdered by them April 21, while thus a captive for ten days. With the prospect of death ever before him, he thought of others, rather than of himself. He refused to purchase his own safety by their peril and met his fate in the spirit of his own latest words – We must trust to God that we may die bravely as Englishmen should do".'

At the transept they turned left and walked, through the south door, into the snow and sunshine.

'I know what you're thinking,' said his wife. 'You're thinking it's a pity that there aren't a lot more like him in racing. But things are improving aren't they? Nothing like so bad as they used to be.'

'Well, we had that Marquess of Ailesbury business not long ago. Why did he have to get up to his tricks at Knavesmire? There's one blessing, though, we've never had to deal with that reprobate "Squire" fellow, Baird. He knows better than to come to York. The racing's above his standard anyway.'

'Morning Mr and Mrs Melrose. I'm glad to see you still have him toeing the line Madam. On the dot every morning.'

James Melrose donned his top hat with one hand and raised his cane with the other – the latter movement a sure indication that he'd suddenly remembered something extremely interesting.

'Do you know where that phrase comes from – toeing the line? Next time you come to a meeting at York, look at that old stone flag just outside the

The Grandstand 1865.

entrance to the old grandstand. That was used, one hundred and fifty years ago, together with a standard measure, for measuring the height of horses. At that time handicapping was by height and age. The stone is six feet four inches by three feet three inches and if you look closely, you'll see two lines cut into it, about five feet apart. Each line is two feet long. The horse had to stand on these lines and, being handicapped according to height, spread its legs out to the ends of the two-feet lines. So I think that this sort of flagstone in racing gave rise to the saying – toe the mark.'

'Interesting, Mr Melrose, very interesting. By the way, you're doing wonders up at the racecourse Mr Melrose. Is it correct that you're having a lot of alterations up there this year?'

'Absolutely correct. We're altering the grand and county stands considerably. We're building a new stand, we're having a new enclosure and we're getting a decent weighing room. Oh, by the way, there's a lot more prize money this year – nearly five thousands pounds in August!'

James Melrose relapsed into thought as the couple made their way home. After a few minutes silence he rested his cane on his shoulder, and then began lecturing the air with it, each movement emphasising a particular word: 'The spirit of amateurism must be maintained of course. It establishes the ideals without which any form of social life is debased. The Turf is greatly supported by the aristocracy, but when that same aristocracy becomes dissolute – and this has been more than apparent at York this century – then what is now termed "professionalism" must take a hand.

'I would hate to see professionals controlling our racing. But if the so-called "lovers" of the Turf are satisfied to see their sport degraded through their own lack of commitment they can have little grievance if the public fails to sympathise. We need the best of professionalism combined with the amateur spirit. But that is a combination for which we must wait a long time I feel. It probably won't occur in my lifetime.

'In the meantime the corporation is hinting that the course should be run by the town. Nonsense, of course, but they're envious of the control over its racing that Doncaster has.

'It will help us to resist such pressure if we can show, quite clearly, that our way of running racing at York is the best in the country. And we won't do that by encouraging characters like the Marquess of Ailesbury.'

15

The Marquess of Ailesbury in Disgrace

Everitt had looked the nearest possible thing to a racing certainty when the Marquess of Ailesbury entered him for the Harewood Plate at York in 1887.

The spectators' joy was unrestrained as they saw their fancy cruising home in the closing stages, his jockey, Martin, apparently needing to demand nothing of him, absolutely nothing.

But the cheers changed to shouts of consternation, the consternation became anxiety and the anxiety grew into fury, as Martin continued to do absolutely nothing, despite the fact that fellow jockey Calder, winner of that year's Ebor Handicap on Silence, was rapidly reducing the gap between Everitt and Whittington.

Martin continued to be oblivious of the existence of Whittington right up to the finishing line, when Calder managed to dead heat.

As Martin returned to the weighing room he faced a mob who were out for his blood. Frustrated punters, fists clenched, rushed towards him. But so, fortunately for Martin, did the police, who formed a protective cordon around him – a cordon which could not, however, protect him from a hail of verbal abuse.

The stewards that day included Lord Durham, the extremely straight-talking Turf administrator, who had no hesitation in summoning Martin before them.

'What was all that nonsense about?' said Durham.

Martin explained that he thought he had won.

'Then let's see how the re-run goes', said Lord Durham. He already had his suspicions of Ailesbury who had been involved in another fishy race at York the previous year.

Martin, by now far more impressed by the stewards' suspicions than he was by Ailesbury's instructions, made very sure that he won the re-run, confirming what the bulk of onlookers already knew.

'Right, let's have Ailesbury and that trainer of his, Tyler, in here,' said Lord Durham. 'But, first of all, I want another word with that jockey.'

Back came Martin, by now seeking a convenient hole in the ground in which to hide.

'Now then Martin,' said Lord Durham. 'There's no need to be frightened.

If you've been coerced at all, or if you've been subjected to dishonest instructions now is the time to own up. Your loyalty now is to your profession and to the sport you serve, not to those who might seek, unscrupulously, to use you. Did Mr Tyler instruct you to lose on Everitt?'

The truth tumbled from Martin's lips. He poured out a full confession which included a similar incident in the Great Yorkshire Handicap at York the previous year.

'Are you referring to the race in which you rode Gallinule?' asked Durham. 'As I remember it, Gallinule came second in the Great Yorkshire Handicap. What happened on that occasion?'

'His Lordship himself told me not to win at York that day,' stammered Martin.

Martin was told not to worry, that he had done wrong, but that it was through a misconception of loyalty. He would, however, be receiving a reprimand.

Durham was furious that Ailesbury's tricks had been allowed to continue at York after the Gallinule affair. On that occasion someone stated that they had heard the marquess tell Martin not to win. It was then indelicate to press any allegation, since the evidence was uncorroborated and since the running of that race had not been so obviously crooked. But here was Ailesbury again, making his deception obvious and the racing ludicrous.

Ailesbury walked into the stewards' room without uttering a word to anyone, the customary devil-may-care attitude noticeably missing. Lord Durham stood impassively before him, the two other stewards – the Hon W Fitzwilliam and Mr R Vyner – sitting tight-lipped and intense on either side of him.

Durham threw protocol to the winds. 'The game's up Ailesbury, we know what's happened. Do you deny you told Tyler that Martin wasn't to win this race?'

'If that is what is alleged, then who am I to deny it? I imagine that this must give you some pleasure. It has always been obvious that you in the Jockey Club don't like me. The feeling, however, is quite mutual. You're either pompous, like yourself Durham, or stupid old bores.'

'Is it true that you instructed Martin not to win last year's Great Yorkshire Handicap, on this same course, when he was on Gallinule?'

'It could be. I really can't remember such trivia.'

'Ailesbury, you will hear more of this later. May I say how painful it is that a man with your rank in life should indulge in such conduct. You are very young, admittedly, but that is little excuse for shunning the company of your fellow peers in order to mix with men who bring discredit to the Turf – men of the lowest possible character. On your way out please ask your trainer Tyler to come in.'

Ailesbury shrugged his shoulders, gave a contemptuous smile and sauntered from the room.

Shortly afterwards both the Marquess of Ailesbury and Tyler were

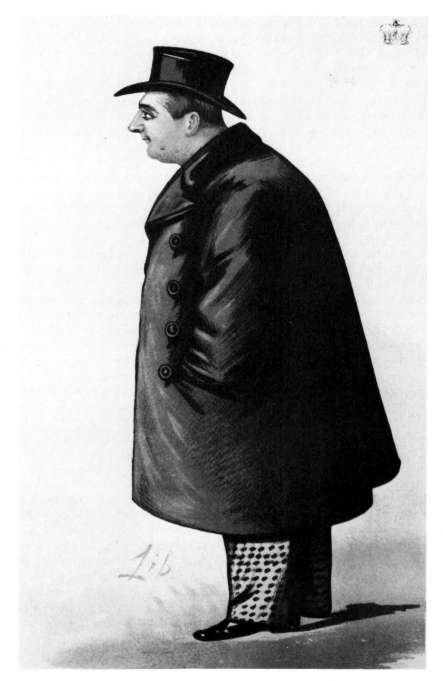

The Marquess of Ailesbury from a contemporary caricature.

warned off – a heavy slur for anyone in the Turfing world to bear, and one which no other of Ailesbury's station in life had suffered previously, or has suffered since. The indictment was all the more regrettable as Ailesbury's grandfather had been the proud owner of several good racehorses.

When the Marquess sold his horse, Gallinule, which Martin had ridden in the Great Yorkshire Handicap on Knavesmire, it went to a 'Mr Abington' for five thousand, one hundred guineas. 'Mr Abington' was the Turf name used by George Alexander Baird, a rich, indulged, prank-playing young reprobate, who managed to get himself warned off for two years for foul riding.

Baird, whose main preoccupation in life was to squander a huge fortune on gambling, women and rabble-rousing, was a fine horseman who, nevertheless, steered clear of York as he, and others like him, couldn't make the weights there.

Baird, whose entourage included prize-fighters and social vultures, frequently behaved like a lout, playing crude jokes and intimidating those who resisted. It was obvious that Durham placed Ailesbury in much the same mould as Baird.

Durham, indeed, would dog those who threatened to bring the Turf into disrepute, and had no qualms about making public indictments. But the most telling of all was made in Harker's Hotel, York, the old York Tavern, at the annual Gimcrack Dinner. It was made only weeks after Ailesbury had been warned off. But this time Durham was treading much more dangerous ground, for he was attacking a fellow member of the Jockey Club.

Hands reached for the brandy and teeth took a firmer grip on cigars as Lord Durham launched into Sir George Chetwynd, former senior steward of the Jockey Club, who owned a large string of racehorses, but who relied a lot, probably too much, on betting. It had been well-known that one of his jockeys, Charles Wood, had been pulling horses, probably at Chetwynd's instigation.

Durham, acting in the best interests of the sport, told the hushed, smoke filled room at Harker's about the running of horses at 'certain well-known stables', making it absolutely certain that everyone identified the stables as Sherrard's – the ones in which Chetwynd had an interest.

Chetwynd reacted swiftly and impulsively, challenging Durham to a duel. But Chetwynd was reminded that, even if he won the duel, it would hardly re-establish his honour.

He and Durham, therefore, met head on in a libel action. Both agreed that the case should go before judges with an expert knowledge of racing. In 1889, therefore, it was heard before arbitrators – the Rt Hon James Lowther, the Earl of March and Prince Soltykoff.

Durham charged Chetwynd with pulling horses and, as a member of the Jockey Club, with conniving and with helping Wood to break the rules of racing.

Under cross-examination Chetwynd showed himself to be a professional

Sir George Chetwynd.

punter. Wood was the financial power behind the stables and, when it became illegal for jockeys to own horses, he made a sale to Chetwynd which was a mere paper transaction.

Chetwynd was claiming twenty thousand pounds damages, but was awarded a farthing – the standard method of showing contempt for a plaintiff's claim in such cases. He accepted defeat and resigned from the Jockey Club.

123

Turn-of-the-century Knavesmire.

At Knavesmire the fading old lady called the nineteenth century had little to add to the proceedings.

Cheery Jim Fagan rode his second Great Ebor winner, Cassocks Bride, just before the dawn of the twentieth century – yet another feather in the cap of the jockey from William I'Anson's Malton stable. For Jim, who later became a trainer, had also won the Gimcrack Stakes six times within an eleven-year period.

But the first 'Auld Lang Syne' of the new century wished not so much for improved racing on Knavesmire, as for the guarantee that racing would continue there at all . . .

16

A Crisis Averted
Racing remains on Knavesmire

Racing on Knavesmire was doomed. Of that there seemed little doubt. Dapper James Melrose paced the office of the wine and spirits firm which he had founded and recalled that golden day, more than fifty years previously, when he had witnessed the titanic clash between Voltigeur and Flying Dutchman.

He looked down to the carnation he was sporting, slowly removed it and placed it on his desk, almost as if he were laying a wreath on a coffin.

It was September 1902. The Race Committee's lease from the Corporation had at last run out, and their fight to retain control of racing on Knavesmire was beginning to appear futile.

The crisis was caused by pressure from the pasture-masters – their new landlords – most of whom professed little, if any, interest in the future of racing in York.

But the Corporation themselves had more than a passing interest. Only too aware of the position at nearby Doncaster, where civic control was the tradition, their minds were becoming conditioned to taking control in York.

Two groups stood in their way – York Race Committee, who were prepared to take their racing elsewhere rather than let it fall under municipal control, and the pasture-masters, who had deeply entrenched rights over Knavesmire.

The pasture-masters, who tended to view the Race Committee as a privileged, self-indulgent squierarchy with money to burn, were attempting to raise extra, unearned income, by extracting as much rent as they could from the Committee. Their aspirations were fuelled by news from comparatively-modest Pontefract, where the rent had been increased tenfold.

But the last straw was added when the pasture-masters, who paid their own dues to the Corporation in the shape of rates, demanded that the Race Committee should pay the rates as well.

'Mr Melrose, there's Mr Teasdale to see you,' called a clerk as he pushed up the partition window.

Teasdale – just the man he wanted to see! Dynamic as ever at the age of seventy-four, Melrose prepared to greet John Teasdale, a lawyer who was

Watching the race, fruit seller included, 1905.

also secretary to the York Race Committee. Teasdale more than anyone, appreciated just how precarious the position was.

Teasdale removed his gloves with great deliberation as Melrose indicated a seat.

'Well, what was the outcome of last night's meeting?' asked Melrose.

'The pasture-masters have delivered an ultimatum,' replied Teasdale slowly. 'If we do manage to obtain a further lease from the Corporation we must pay rates on that area of Knavesmire which we occupy. If we don't agree within a month then negotiations will be ended.'

'There's no possibility of a compromise?'

'None.'

There was a long, thoughtful pause.

'Do they have a point?' ventured Melrose. 'We do occupy space over which they could otherwise graze their beasts. Their demands are becoming unreasonable, and their tone leaves much to be desired. But are they correct in principle? The *Yorkshire Post* seems to think that we are being obstinate.'

'The *Yorkshire Post* doesn't have our problem to deal with.' Teasdale's voice bore an edge of irritation. 'If the pasture-masters were to exploit the area which the course occupies, the grazing benefits would be negligible.

'But this really isn't the point,' he continued. 'A lease under such conditions would be intolerable. Confident development and planning are difficult enough without the Corporation taking an uncomfortable interest in Knavesmire. To have the added frustration of unpredictable demands by the Freemen of York – the pasture-masters – makes our prospects on Knavesmire black indeed.

'Remember, too, that the Jockey Club's demands for improvements grow year by year. We must increase our stakes on behalf of owners, and meetings of the quality which we run can't possibly stand the additional drain on their resources which the pasture-masters could cause.'

'I do understand Mr Teasdale.' Melrose was vexed at having appeared compromising. 'I simply find it regrettable that a greater spirit of harmony cannot exist between the town and its own racecourse.'

Teasdale nodded his head understandingly.

'Your sympathies, as the devoted, long-serving chairman of our committee are to be admired Mr Melrose. You are a former Lord Mayor of the City, and take a deep interest in many York organisations.

'But the fact is Mr Melrose that your attitude to, and affection for, the traditions of York racing are shared by few of your city colleagues.

'To put it bluntly the Corporation is in no justifiable position to identify itself, directly at least, with York Racecourse.

'The support for York racing comes, as it always has, from the county. Its roots are in the enthusiasm of the Yorkshire gentry, however misguided such enthusiasm might have been at times.

'York stands almost alone as a meeting run on the old lines. Its very traditions appear odd to the city businessman who can see the main object of racing merely in terms of dividends.'

'Must the city inevitably control racing on Knavesmire if it is to survive?' asked Jimmy Melrose.

'No. The committee, as you know, enjoys great support in the county, and I doubt if the Jockey Club would grant a licence to any meeting with the Corporation as its managers. Remember, too, that the Corporation does not own the land on which we have our six-furlong course. So they would be unable to control the six-furlong course.

'We have other sites in mind, as you know, and our traditional support would follow us wherever we went. But if we moved, and Knavesmire died, the city would indeed suffer. That is one of the cards I am playing.'

'You mean you have other cards up your sleeve?' Melrose's eyes began to twinkle.

'Yes. I'm damned if we should give up without a fight. Racing belongs on Knavesmire – our kind of racing. This isn't Doncaster. The Corporation are finding the pasture-masters something of a stumbling block as well....' Teasdale's tone was becoming more emotive.

'So?'

'So ... we might be able to persuade the Corporation that it is as much in their interests as ours that they should buy out the rights of the pasture-masters.'

128

Members of the Race Committee, spring 1908. Left to right: *Viscount Downe, The Hon H W Fitzwilliam, James Melrose, John Teasdale.*

129

The carriage park in Edwardian days.

'Impossible. That would mean a special Act of Parliament.' Melrose lowered his head in disappointment.

Teasdale rose to his feet, took up his gloves and cane and walked to the door. Before opening it, he paused, turned towards Melrose and winked.

'Precisely, Mr Melrose. Precisely.'

Months later James Melrose was carrying out another routine inspection of his wines, spirits and premises. It was a pink orchid day, one for which Melrose held mixed feelings. Spring was in the air, but the prospects of a spring race meeting in that year of 1903 appeared remote.

There was one blessing: several prospective sites for a course had been found, one of which happened to be quite near Knavesmire. And, wherever York races chose to settle, they had the full support of the racing community. Assurances to that effect had been pouring in.

He picked up the latest edition of the *Yorkshire Herald*, from which comforting words sprang, 'If, as is possible, existing arrangements may be altered, it will not be the Race Committee that will be to blame, but those who, imagining there is a source of wealth that does not exist, have put pressure to bear on the committee.

'It has been said that the Corporation wishes to see itself in the same

Race crowds 1913; there are at least five enclosures, most of which have now disappeared.

position that Doncaster Corporation is with respect to the Doncaster meeting. If such an ambitious notion has entered the mind of any member of the Corporation the sooner it is dismissed the better.

'York Corporation has never been prominent in its support of the races, either on Clifton Ings or on Knavesmire, and it has never had any practical control of the management.

'On the other hand, Doncaster races, as far back as 1616, and presumably earlier, were fostered and controlled by the Corporation. York, on the contrary, has always been under the management of Yorkshire gentlemen.

'It is to be doubted whether the Jockey Club would grant their licence to any other meeting with a Corporation as its managers.'

Yes, it was comforting to know that the support was there, but how long would it take effectively to re-establish racing in York? Melrose doubted if it would come to fruition in his lifetime.

With a dignified clatter, the partition window flew up again. 'Mr Teasdale is on the telephone Mr Melrose.'

'Good Morning Mr Teasdale. What dire tidings do you bear this morning? ... You've managed to work something out with the Corporation? ... You sound exuberant to say the least ... Hazard a guess you say? I haven't the faintest idea ... What Act of Parliament? ... Oh that Act of Parliament!'

The pink in James Melrose's orchid faded into comparative obscurity as an exuberant crimson lit up his face and spread to his ear-lobes. As Teasdale continued his tele-communicated report Melrose hopped from one foot to another with excitement.

'Magnificent, Mr Teasdale, magnificent! Yes indeed, the fighting is not over yet but we have borrowed some valuable time.'

As he replaced the ear-piece, Melrose chuckled with admiration for the enterprising Teasdale. With the Corporation intending to buy out the free-men's interest in Knavesmire this left only one opponent. This also meant the likelihood of a further lease – sufficient time, possibly, in which to consolidate his position, and to gain enough prestige to resist any further demands.

Melrose turned to one of his young clerks. 'This calls for a special celebration. I will open one of our very special ports.'

Four years of cautious optimism followed; four years of negotiation and re-negotiation; four years of town politics, of Westminster discussions, of legal complexities. At last the Act was passed. The pasture masters pocketed their cash, and surrendered their rights.

In 1907 James Melrose, red rose in buttonhole, stood up to address a meeting of his committee: 'Gentlemen, we can now increase the paddock,

The winner's enclosure, 1913.

Great Air Race, Yorkshire v Lancashire held on Knavesmire October 1913.

add to our enclosures, rail in and manage the track and, last by no means least, have sole control of Knavesmire during race weeks.'

'We have been granted a lease of thirty-five years, the expiration of which I certainly shall not see. Our position should now be stronger. The war is far from finished, but a major battle has been won.'

17

Between the Wars-A New Era

 The real, terrible war, was dragging towards its long-awaited end. On an airfield in England a young man called Leslie Petch, son of a Yorkshire farmer and hunt enthusiast, was facing a test as a fledgling pilot with the Royal Flying Corps, which was soon to change its name to the Royal Air Force.

'Right Petch, no trouble, no complications. Just remember that, although you may be tempted to think otherwise, this machine is not a horse and will respond only to directions and not, repeat not, to exhortations. No dramatics please, let's just have a simple, straightforward flight. Remember exactly what I've taught you and we are faced with a mere formality. I'm not going to bother watching; just stroll around to the mess afterwards and we'll go through the rituals.'

Petch was going solo for the first time ... officially that was. The nonchalant instructor stepped well away from the aircraft as Petch nodded his apparent understanding of instructions.

The engine belched and spluttered like an addicted smoker greeting a new day as the instructor pulled a cigarette-holder from his pocket, fumbled a flaking paper-covered conglomeration of tobacco into base, lit up and thrust his hands together, in a nervous Napoleonic grasp behind his greatcoat.

While Petch revelled at the opportunity to gain total control of the shuddering biplane, ground staff yanked the chocs away after spinning the machine's whiskers into life.

The aeroplane snorted forwards, sniffed at the ground, from which it was soon to depart and rolled expectantly along the primitive runway. Groaning with ever increasing rapidity, it reared its snout away from the earth and clawed skywards, the instructor pacing along behind, as though wishing to impart some extra force to the effort.

'Is that Petch?' The instructor had company.

'Yes, my last one today, thank God. Should be straightforward. Inclined to be impulsive this one. But there again, aren't we all at some time or other? Good luck to him anyway, if he's going to finish up over there. You know, sometimes I fell as though I'm churning out sausages for some gullet that's never satisfied. I mean, which way, for example, is this one going?'

'Vertically, by the looks of things,' observed his companion.

The instructor gazed in horror as the aircraft intensified its snarl, stood on its tail and clawed upwards. The machine held its breath, lay on its back and snarled back to life, completing the most unexpected of loops.

Petch completed his solo effort in peaceful and conventional style. As the aircraft taxied gently back the instructor launched into a tirade. 'I told him not to tackle anything fancy – just bloody showing off that was, looping the loop indeed! We've no place for that sort of thing. Who the hell does he think he is? I'll give him looping the loop . . .'

The grin of triumph was evident on young Petch's face as the instructor stormed forward, tagged closely by his companion.

'Go easy', advised the companion. 'At least he showed some enterprise. It might come in handy some day . . .'

Victoria Alexandra Alice Mary, the Princess Royal, aunt of Queen Elizabeth II, made her way to the paddock at York races to watch the saddling for the Lowther Handicap. She was distinctively dressed in a costume of white silk, edged with deep green embroidery, her large, white crepe-de-chine hat being trimmed with a lace scarf.

It was a mellow, drowsy afternoon in August 1922. Princess Mary and her husband, Viscount Lascelles, had motored over from Harewood House in West Yorkshire to watch the racing on Gimcrack Day.

It was a day for fashions, a day for reminiscing, but a day of repressed sadness. The enclosures murmured politely, but there were few roars from the course. Too many gaps in the ranks perhaps.

There was a trace of resentment in the air too. When Jack Smith looked across at the complacent inner enclosures he wondered what he was doing here. These races weren't for him. It was Toffs' Day at York. The crowd wasn't a racing community, it was a racing club. Ebor Day was all right, more of a day for the lads. But still, after that rotten war, you'd think that the ordinary bloke would get a better deal.

Nobody cares, thought Jack Smith, a man unaccustomed to malice. But, socially, these were not the best times to be objective. As Jack flickered his resentful eye around the groups of the comfortable, he failed to notice two diminutive figures who were rapt in conversation. Occasionally they paused to roar with laughter or to slap each other on the back.

They were two old codgers – James Melrose, still permutating the button-hole display, and Johnny Osborne, the jockey who had ridden nine Gimcrack winners between 1863 and 1880. They were delightfully old, and enjoying every eternity of it.

'Mind you,' said Melrose, 'We've a long way to go yet. Look over there, by the rails. They're in a world apart. They must think that we don't care.'

James Melrose was ninety-four years old, had been presiding at Gimcrack Club dinners for some fifty years, and had been chairman of the Race Committee for about the same length of time. He felt that he had reached his limit.

James Melrose with H.M. Queen Mary and H.R.H. The Princess Royal.

John Osborne, the rider of nine Gimcrack winners between 1863 and 1880, seen here with Dobson Peacock c 1920.

'You must miss Mrs Melrose,' said Osborne.

Melrose changed the subject. 'You know the old saying about 'toeing the line'. Did I ever tell you about its origin? At least, this is my theory . . .'

'Yes, the slab and the marks, you did tell me,' said Osborne. 'But you were talking about not caring.'

'Well,' said Melrose, 'We have gone through a terrible war, and yet we are further apart. I think this must be my last year as chairman here, and I'm so pleased that we've made so much progress. We've regained a lot of prestige, and the County Race Balls are flourishing again. But prestige in itself is not enough. Enterprise is needed to bring the racing public together.'

They looked across the course, which so recently had borne the marks of military occupation, both by the Army and by the Royal Air Force. The Race Committee had received compensation for the scars, but some old wounds still smarted.

The running of the Gimcrack that afternoon was to be a memorable one. Lord Woolavington, who had already won the Derby with Captain Cuttle, was out to complete a prestigious double with Town Guard. He made it, his horse winning easily in a canter. The enclosures warmed to the odds-on winner. The stands stood politely and the fashions resumed their intertwining. But the cries from the course were feeble . . .

The Princess Royal returned the following spring to the racecourse where

A group of well-known jockeys of the 1920s and 1930s. Left to right *Steve Donoghue, Joe Child, Fred Fox and 'Brownie' Carslake.*

she felt at home. The pull of the summer meeting was again irresistible, but the rain threw a cloak over Ebor Day. As the crowds filtered away, Steve Donoghue prepared himself for the last race on the card – the Duke of York Stakes, run over a mile and a quarter for three-year-olds.

By the time he had mounted the Derby winner, Papyrus, thousands had already conceded that the weather was the winner and were beating a damp, hasty retreat. They missed one of the greatest finishes that Knavesmire had

Brown Jack (Steve Donoghue up) after winning the Ebor Handicap 1931.

experienced. Steve and Papyrus pulled out all the stops against Mr A H Straker's Craig Eleyr, but were beaten by a short head, with only a head separating Papyrus and Lord Astor's Concertina.

But Papyrus won the day. Craig Eleyr was disqualified for boring and not keeping a straight course.

Harry Wragg, Gordon Richards, Steve Donoghue, Tommy Weston, Willy Carr, Dick Perryman, Freddy Fox – names which evoke those wistful, days of the twenties and thirties – counted victories at York as triumphs.

Richards made a distinctive mark on Knavesmire's two main events, winning the Ebor four times and revelling in three Gimcrack victories in the years between the debilitating two world wars.

Donoghue, the working man's favourite, particularly when partnering Brown Jack, brought a smile to many a face when, on Brown Jack, he carried off the 1931 Ebor. Steve followed this with a Silver Jubilee Year success on Sir Victor Sassoon's Museum.

While the cream of the racing world converged upon Knavesmire, the Race Committee lived under the ever-imminent threat of being milked by a Corporation take-over.

Little by little, improvements were being nudged in, like wagons being shyly pushed from a railway siding. But sweeping changes, so often envisaged, had to be shelved until that hypothetical day when the threat would be lifted. There could be no investment without security.

In 1926 the Race Committee aimed to revive the Yorkshire Cup over the full two miles of the course – a throwback to the early nineteenth century when the hunting men of Yorkshire held their central meeting on Knavesmire. This was not a good year to choose as social grievances and disparities in a far-from-merry England found grim expression in the general strike. The spring meeting was cancelled.

The following spring was a different matter, Tommy Weston winning the revived event on Templestowe, a gelding owned by a former steward at York, Colonel Hugh Stobbart. The colonel lived in nearby Middlethorpe Hall, quite a way from the collieries of Durham in which he had considerable interests. The atmosphere of these years could, indeed, be a little brooding. In some way an affinity had to be created between those who appeared to have so much and those who definitely had too little.

A young man who, as a youth, had driven his flying instructor to the brink of a heart attack by looping the loop on his first solo, perused an advertisement which had been placed by the steeplechase committee at Wetherby Racecourse, a few miles from York.

An auctioneer was needed, and Leslie Petch, son of a North Yorkshire farmer, point-to-point rider and, more pertinently, racecourse auctioneer, considered himself eminently suitable for the job.

He applied, and his appointment appeared to be a mere formality. 'We would like you to take the job,' the committee chairman told him, 'and, naturally, act as judge during racing.'

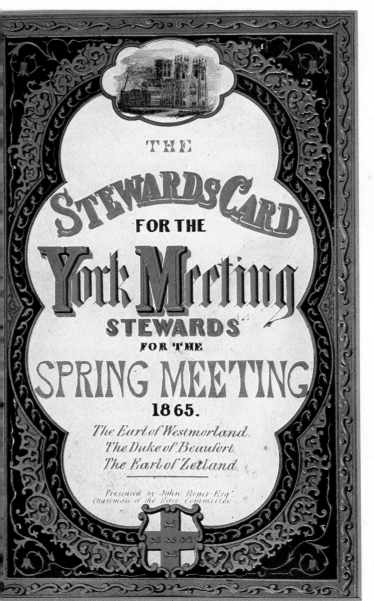

Stewards' card 1865 and passes for various enclosures. (York Racing Museum)

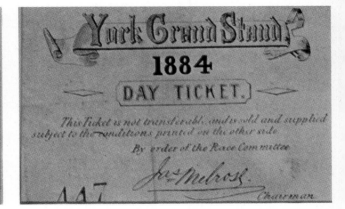

Looking across the course towards the grandstand. (Fred Spencer)

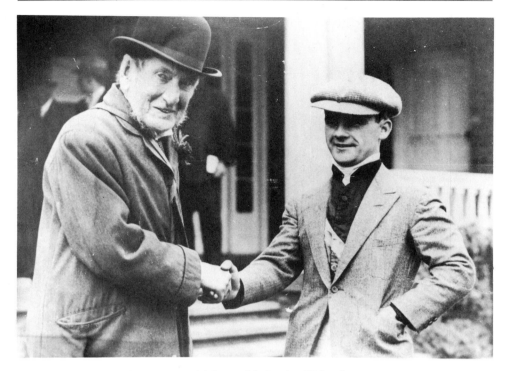

James Melrose with Gordon Richards.

'Act as what?'

'As judge. The appointment does, as you probably know, involve being race judge. There's no problem there, obviously.'

'Naturally, obviously, well of course . . . only too pleased.'

Petch had reacted on impulse again. But now he needed to use his enterprise. Back home at the farm he telephoned seasoned judge and racing pundit Major Fairfax-Blakeborough: 'Look, I wonder if you could help . . . I've never judged before . . . could you come and give me a hand . . .?'

At about the same time that Leslie Petch was being introduced to Yorkshire racing, a familiar figure was about to take his leave of it.

James Melrose was wearing a white carnation to mark a very special occasion. On the table before him a huge cake bore a hundred tiny candles, one for every year of his life. Taking a long knife, he cleaved out the first slice – an act which was greeted with warm applause from those who stood in the long crowded room at his home.

That morning he had attended a special service of thanksgiving in his honour. In a few days time he would be attending the August meeting at Knavesmire.

Letters and telegrams were piled in tottering stacks. Friends streamed through the house, exchanging best wishes for sherry, port or something stronger.

For once James Melrose was stuck for words as a friend raised one message high above the babble of heads and called for silence.

'I have here, ladies and gentlemen, a very special message, which I think you would all like to hear. It is sent from His Majesty's Yacht Victoria and Albert and reads:

"Knowing that on Sunday, August 5, 1928, you will attain the age of one hundred, I desire to offer you my warmest congratulations.

"Yours has indeed been not only a long, but a useful life of true citizenship and of devotion to your native and beloved city, which you have served in many capacities.

"Your example of patriotism and zeal in well-doing will be an inspiration to the many who hold you in high and affectionate regard, and to future generations of the citizens of York. George Rex".'

James Melrose at the south v north jockeys' football match 1932. South (white shirts) left to right (back) H. Wragg, T. Gardener, R. A. Jones; (middle) G. Richards, C. Smirke, C. Elliott, J. Dines, F. Winter, T. Weston; (front) G. Hulme, R. Perryman. North (black shirts) (back) A. Waudby, J. Thwaites, D. Rushbrook; (middle) J. Taylor, W. Sherry, F. Taylor, A. Jamieson, D. Crisp; (front) J. Nolan, W. Nevett, G. Baines.

Melrose's cheeks were flushed with a combination of exhilaration, emotion and gentle inebriation as hand after hand pumped his forearm up and down.

'We'll no doubt see you kick off the jockeys' football match as usual next year Mr Melrose.'

'Try and stop me. I might not be organising very much these days, but I haven't lost my touch at soccer. Now I wonder if you would all excuse me for a few moments.'

Melrose steered himself confidently towards his study. He felt on top of the world, as fit as a youngster of eighty. He felt like doing a little bit of writing himself. To whom? Well, why not to the citizens of York?

Dipping his pen in the well of Stephen's blue-black ink, he addressed himself to the Lord Mayor:

'Dear Sir, I should like to take this opportunity to thank, from the bottom of my heart, the citizens of York for their most kind congratulations and best wishes on my reaching my one hundredth birthday, which God in his providence has permitted me to do.

'All my thoughts are for this dear old city of my birth, and much of the joy of the present times is derived from the warm friendship of my fellow citizens.'

The Guildhall, meeting place of York City Council, was alive with rumblings, mutterings and accusations. Disorder was imminent. The Lord Mayor's gavel hammered out a demand for quietness and attention, as Councillor A G Watson, chairman of the Parks Committee, rose slowly and gravely to his feet.

'My Lord Mayor,' said Watson, 'On behalf of my committee and myself I must emphatically repudiate suggestions that friction exists between ourselves and the members of York Race Committee.'

'My Lord Mayor', came a cry from the chamber, 'if we're always going to have these debates over the Race Committee's continual applications for improvements, I suggest we might be advised to take over the running of the races ourselves. As far as some of us are concerned friction does exist.'

'My Lord Mayor,' retorted a voice from the opposing ranks, 'This council is no more equipped to run a race meeting than a debating society is to sail an ocean liner. These are the politics of envy. It is very much in the city's interest that the Race Committee's enterprise should be given every support.'

My Lord Mayor's attention was sought from every corner of the room.

'Just to think,' muttered one observer, 'That Jimmy Melrose went to rest only a few months ago, and here we are, going through the same old arguments. We seem to have forgotten the funeral service in the Minster.'

Councillor Watson had the Lord Mayor's attention again.

'The Board of Control wishes to install the new totalisator system at York on a scale parallel to the size and importance of the meeting. This would mean alterations and further buildings. We are the landlords, and the Race

Committee is not prepared to make a substantial increase on its present rental.

'If we cannot agree, the York meetings will fall in status. It is claimed that if the totalisator system, "the Tote" I believe it is called, were not to be installed generally, then the future of racing itself in this country would be imperilled.

'We are now in the year 1929, and the problem is far from being a new one. As I have said, there is no open conflict between ourselves and the Race Committee, but a difficulty certainly exists.'

A new voice made itself heard from the benches: 'We all know, my Lord Mayor, that the Race Committee's present lease has relatively few years to run, and it can hardly be expected that the Board of Control will incur the expense of their elaborate totalisator system on land upon which the security of tenure does not exceed fourteen years.

'Gentlemen, the future of the races at York is at stake. Any profits from the Tote could not go towards increases we might make in rent. The Parks Committee have already recommended that we reject the Race Committee's offer of a limited increase in rent – the difference between that offer and our original demand, being, I believe, a matter of a few hundred pounds.

'I ask you, gentlemen, are we to jeopardise the future of probably the finest racecourse in the land by such quibbling? If this be the source of contention, then let it go to arbitration.

'My Lord Mayor, the provisions of the totalisator buildings at York would involve considerable alterations and expense on the part of the Race Committee. The installation would be one of the largest in the country, and would be accompanied by other substantial improvements, providing far greater comfort and accommodation for the race-going public.

'Remember that there are no shareholders at York, and any profits gained from the racing there are spent on the upkeep of the course and its buildings. We seem not to appreciate, My Lord Mayor, that we have inherited a fine racecourse, in the glory of which we are content to bask. Are we to destroy it for the sake of a few hundred pounds?'

When the Hon Reginald Parker, president of the Gimcrack Dinner, rose to his feet in the Royal Station Hotel that November he had a special announcement to make:

'Only this afternoon we were able to pass plans for the installation of the totalisator. We have been able to come to an arrangement with York Corporation to extend our lease for thirty-five years. But for this extension the Totalisator would never have come to York.

'There is one matter to which I must particularly refer. When the question of the Tote was being discussed in the City Council, one councillor said that, from information he had received, he could not agree with the statement that the Race Committee did not get anything for its activities.

'I have been on the Race Committee for more than forty years, and during

Foxglove II, winner of the 1935 Ebor Handicap, ridden by Gordon Richards.

The famous tipster Prince Monolulu who was a familiar figure at Knavesmire for many years.

that time never has a claim or payment of one single shilling been drawn by the Race Committee from the race fund.

'Some people have an idea that you have to get a bit out of everything you do. I am glad to say that this is not our principle. We may be thankful that there are still sportsmen who are prepared to give their time free and their full energy to promote the great national sport of racing.'

The man who had to supply the champagne at that year's dinner was Sir A Bailey, whose Roral had won the Gimcrack Stakes. The jockey was Dick Perryman, of whom we shall hear later. For Perryman was to be the trainer of a unique victor on Knavesmire – a triumph which was to take place before one of the greatest, and one of the most silent crowds in the history of Knavesmire.

Dick rode home four Gimcrack winners before the outbreak of the Second World War, but his 1934 victory had a double significance. It was aboard Bahram, owned by the Aga Khan. One of the outstanding horses of the twentieth century, Bahram underlined the significance of the Gimcrack Stakes as a race which, apart from possessing a unique dignity and standard, was a racing prophet.

The Gimcrack Stakes had become a classic of the Flat season's sunset – a hint of the great things to come when the sun rose on the following season. Bahram was to win the Derby, 2000 Guineas and St Leger of 1935. The record speaks for itself.

The Gimcrack bore a vintage touch, but the race's connection with champagne was brought to an end in the same year. Any 'hangover' from the old Champagne Stakes, that noble enterprise of the 1830s, was cured. The Aga Khan was the last winning owner to face the forfeit of champagne at the Gimcrack dinner. At about the same time as Adolf Hitler was beginning his rise to power in Germany, champagne was becoming prohibitively expensive in England.

Vaguely apprehensive though the atmosphere was in the later thirties, York races saw little, if any, of the social resentment which had marked the twenties. Race meetings on Knavesmire were treats for the family. On the free course a hefty bet of a sixpence each way was the day's fling for dad, but what a spree for the kids, with roundabouts, sticky toffee apples and ice-cream galore! For a silver three-penny bit you could sacrifice a small packet of Woodbines to have your fortune told by Gipsy Rose Lee. Dutch street organs thumped out the old favourites and jellied eels slithered down many a gullet between races.

'I gotta horse!' was the bellow from near the trainers' entrance as that huge, flamboyantly feathered West Indian tipster, Prince Monolulu, plied his famous trade, pausing a while to perch a child on his shoulders for a snapshot.

But the days were becoming restless and uneasy.

18

World War II

 Charles Ingram Courtenay Wood, a man who, ultimately, would have a profound psychological effect on York Races, spent three years of this disturbingly undisturbed period as a lieutenant in the Royal Horse Guards. It was a peace-time whisper of more dramatic things to come.

His father, Edward, was the statesman Lord Halifax, inheritor of estates at Garrowby, some ten miles from York Racecourse. Garrowby was later to be described by Charles as 'the last bastion'.

Both were tall, angular figures, their inclined heads portraying both an English understatement and a consciousness of their height. Both bore characteristics which one associated with the early Victorian days, when the country squire-tenant relationship was one of the most basic in the land. Both had a deep love of the countryside and both were devoted to the Anglican church.

The Halifax 'aura' can best be captured in the exquisite parish church at Kirby Underdale, which snuggles cosily into the gentle hills of the Yorkshire Wolds – a church at which Prince Charles, Prince of Wales, was to attend Sung Eucharist in the 1970s.

When Charles Wood first left the Army, in 1937, he was elected Member of Parliament for York. But his heart, one feels, lay elsewhere than in politics.

His father, a more aloof figure than Charles, became Foreign Secretary . . . and what a time he picked! For in 1938 it befell the lot of Edward Wood, Lord Halifax, Foreign Secretary under Chamberlain, to negotiate with Adolf Hitler, Chancellor of the German Reich. Edward's detachment, which could place him in an unreal world, also enabled him to put the devilishly devious Hitler in a reasonable light.

Hitler, observed Edward, was very much alive, his eyes, which he was surprised to see were blue, moved about all the time (like a swaying cobra?): 'The play of emotion – sardonic humour, scorn, something almost wistful – is rapid. He struck me as very sincere, and as believing everything he said . . .'

Wishful thinking indeed, and one which hardly endeared Lord Halifax to Churchill!

But the former Viceroy of India, who had never quite fathomed Gandhi

Edward Wood, Earl of Halifax from the portrait by Sir Oswald Birley.

Charles Wood, Earl of Halifax painted by B. R. Linklater.

either, was appointed by Winston as American Ambassador at a crucial period in the lonely days of early 1941.

It was the last year of peace, and as the August meeting opened at York military vehicles were rumbling to and fro, like stage-hands prematurely whisking away the scenery for another show.

The cheers were tinged with sadness as Gordon Richards rode Prince Aly Khan's Tant Mieux to victory in the Gimcrack.

A few days later Prime Minister Chamberlain announced to the nation that Hitler had refused to accept the ultimatum made by the British and French. It was war.

On Knavesmire an army lorry pulled up, disgorging a party of paratroopers. 'Get fell in!' yelled the sergeant. Before them floated an anchored elephant, silver and fat with its ears in its tail. Beneath it, and attached to it, was a large basket.

'Right lads, this is it – the static from a balloon, a very pregnant balloon. This jump is the worst one: very nasty, but after this everything is easy. Those who prefer to die should take one smart step forward . . . no takers . . . good. First section . . .!'

Now it was the real war . . . with a vengeance. No heroics, just bloody suffering. The beaches of Dunkirk seethed with a murmuring, coughing, sweating, demoralised mass of humanity – the remains of the British Expeditionary Force. Shells pounded here, there, everywhere.

'Heads down!' Arms scratched pitiful holes in the sand, but if you tried to be an ostrich you would get your backside blown off. Lie flat, so flat that you disappear.

Yet another fighter coming in low. Everyone went down, like so many dominoes. Ears were covered; that was a sure way of stopping the bullets. Count to ten. Look up, then stand up – slowly. Check that you're in one piece. Somebody's moaning, somebody's crying. Thank God it's not you.

Leslie Petch, an officer in the Green Howards infantry, checked on his men. Not far away yelling, choking, screaming men were fighting through the water, their arms desperately extended towards boats already groaning under the weight of troops.

One of his men seemed to be shouting something at him. But he couldn't hear a thing for a damned ringing in his ears.

It was a cool night in April 1942. The city of York was sleeping uneasily, aware that every medieval gable, every terrace, every church spire stood out clearly in the milky light of a 'bomber's moon'. The Minster's towers formed a noble, silvery outline – an imposing invitation to the Luftwaffe.

The British had bombed Lubeck, a dignified cathedral city in northern Germany. Hitler's response was to scan the Baedeker Guide Book – a must for pre-war Germans who were touring England. Historical cities with a three-star rating, York predominating, were to be bombed in reprisal. Bath and Norwich had already been hit. When were they coming to York? The Ack-Ack was supposed to be on its way to Knavesmire. But when, oh when, would it arrive?

Feld-Webel Hans Fruehauf, observer-gunner in a Junkers 88, gazed down, fascinated, at the view below him. Fruehauf was in the leading aircraft of the first wave of bombers to groan, unmolested, through the night. Ahead, basking in tranquillity, was a huge, solidly buttressed church. Substantial though it was, he could have leaned forward and picked it up.

Behind the Junkers rumbled the slower, heavier wave of Heinkel 111s. The raid was on.

Below, in the Bar Convent School, a quarter of a mile from the racecourse, the nuns of the Institute of the Blessed Virgin Mary heard the wail of the sirens. They had heard this sound more than seven hundred times before. But there was also a droning, an unfamiliar one, its rhythm far different from that generated by the Halifax or Wellington bombers.

The ground shook to a series of thuds as the nuns shepherded all the children to the safety of the long narrow cellar, lined on each side with mattresses.

'Sister Bernard. We must fetch Sister Bernard!'

Lying in the infirmary wing of the convent school was an elderly nun, Sister Bernard McLoughlin. Apart from being ill she was rather deaf.

Sisters Agnes Clayton and Andrew Creaghan scampered out of the cellar and down the narrow passage leading to the east wing. Hurrying upstairs they found Sister Bernard still in bed. Realising that it was too dangerous to move her from the wing, they put her under the bed and made their way back.

As they did so, a delayed-action, high-explosive bomb tore through the roof and first floor, finishing up in the laundry cellar. Sister Agnes, running from Sister Bernard's room, was unaware of the trap ahead. Down she fell, through the hole created by the bomb.

As she lay on the menacingly-ticking instrument of death, her leg broken, she looked up to see Sister Andrew, now peering anxiously down from the edge of the gaping hole.

The ticking seemed to grow in volume – a clock of doom, in total, dispassionate control.

'I'm coming down,' shouted Sister Andrew.

'No, don't', pleaded Sister Agnes. 'It's too dangerous. Get an A.R.P. warden.'

Sister Andrew gingerly edged her way along a narrow floorboard next to the skirting board, a strip which the bomb had spared, before speeding on her vital errand.

In the meantime the other nuns heard Sister Agnes crying for help. Out dashed Sisters Gerard McLorry, Patricia O'Connor, Vincent Jordon and Brendan Murphy. When they had almost reached the laundry, everything went blank.

The maids and secular staff in the community cellar found themselves buried in debris. Elsewhere, dazed nuns gradually realised that their black apparel had been torn from their bodies.

The following day they found what remained of Sisters Patricia, Vincent and Brendan. The remnants of Sister Gerard were uncovered on the fifth

An aerial view of Knavesmire, showing the prisoner-of-war huts in the foreground.

day and pieces of Sister Agnes on the sixth.

Sister Bernard, concern for whom gave rise to the grim sequence survived. The force of the explosion hurled a large cupboard onto her bed, forming a shelter from the debris. And, miraculously, the floor of her room held. Sister Bernard died of natural causes in 1959.

Sister Andrew? She is still at the convent, although she has retired from teaching. Her hair is white. It turned white on April 29, 1942.

The anti-aircraft guns were on their way to Knavesmire. They were to arrive a few days later, to be followed by 'Dad's Army' – the Home Guard.

In the meantime they were taking stock after the Baedeker Raid on York. The weirdest things had occurred. Admiral Fairfax, a resplendent clock-figure in the city centre, had his coat-tails burned, but stuck to his post while buildings disintegrated around him. Elsewhere a tin of treacle was bounced all the way round a child's room, forming a bizarre drapery as it mixed with the soot.

Seventy-nine people died in the raid, and two hundred and thirty-eight were injured.

'Dig for victory' was still one of the great catch-phrases when a column of Army three-tonners rumbled up to Knavesmire. Tommies in battle-dress took the pegs from the tail-boards and shouted instructions. Down jumped a stream of figures dressed in dark blue. They were muttering, with needless apprehension, in German. Crews from captured U-boats and enemy merchant vessels, they were heading for the best years of their wartime lives.

As they stretched their legs they took stock of what looked strangely like a racecourse. But, of course, it couldn't be. There was a huge, railed horseshoe, in the middle of which grew grain, potatoes, corn and sugar beet.

The mariners were led towards what appeared to be a grandstand. But of course, it couldn't be. Whoever heard of prisoners-of-war being held at a racecourse?

They would soon get to know the meaning of 'digging for victory'. Each day they would leave the racecourse to help put something into the British war effort – by working on unimaginably receptive farms. For not until the war's end would the horrors perpetuated by their ex-employers be revealed.

As the war drew to its close Charles Ingram Courtenay Wood, Lord Irwin, was still serving as captain with the Horse Guards in the Middle East, where he had been for most of the war. Major Leslie Petch had been invalided out of the Army, through the shattering effects of Dunkirk.

The significant point was that they had both survived. Thousands of miles apart though they then were, these two Yorkshiremen would join forces, bringing racing at York to the heights which it had so often promised – the unbeatable combination of the relaxed country squire and the sharp, bustling entrepreneur.

19

York's St Leger
A memorable post-war classic

 The war was over. There had been no racing on Knavesmire for six years, and the military had left their mark. But the rain encouraged the grass to turn green again in front of the grandstand, and caring workmen planted flowers which evoked a whisper of the pre-war days.

The track itself had never been damaged, and it was evident, in that April of 1945, that racing in the early autumn was more than possible.

The entire city revelled at the news that Knavemire was to stage the first post-war classic, the St Leger, which could not return to its native Doncaster because of unsuitable conditions there. The race was scheduled for September 5th, the second day of the first meeting since hostilities.

Local businessmen rubbed their hands. Hotels were booked up months before the event, not only in York, but in neighbouring towns too. The return of peace, however, found no change in the character of some townspeople, who attempted to exploit the public's yearning for sport by charging outrageous prices for bed and breakfast. Dick Turpin, it was alleged bitterly, rode again. Only the style of robbery differed.

Restaurant and cafe owners, gleefully anticipating the bonanza, soon realised that the end of hell did not mean the beginning of their materialistic heaven. They complained bitterly when the Ministry of Food refused them licences for rationed foods to cope with the crowds.

Manny Shinwell, the Minister of Fuel, threw a damp squib on the corporation's request for the city to be lit up during the three days of racing. Joyful though the meeting might be, ruled Shinwell, it hardly ranked with the final overthrow of the Axis powers by the Allies. 'Conditions for the Victory over Japan celebrations were exceptional,' Shinwell told the corporation.

The corporation had wished to take advantage of the meeting to stage additional peace celebrations, using the same mass of lights which had festooned the city during the VJ festivities.

A sport-starved public now turned to Knavesmire. A period was beginning during which any significant British sporting event was viewed with awe. Top sportsmen, unspoiled by the lavish cash sums which were to be demanded by their successors in later years, were more individualistic and,

The scene at Knavesmire, 5 September 1945, when the St Leger was run there.

generally, more dedicated. The cynicism of the ultra-professional and the blasé attitude of the pampered armchair spectator had yet to come.

The professionals of those wartime years had been members of the forces, using their leave to provide a touch of nostalgia, or coal-miners who turned up at the field of play with their pit-muck still on.

What racing there had been during the war was negligible, so the task of estimating the crowd at this first post-war classic was an impossible one. Well before the meeting hundreds of people camped out on the course.

Excursions rolled in from all parts of the country, recalling the days of those great Knavesmire challenge matches. Eventually the course resembled a tent-town, festooned with elaborate canopies and improvised verandahs.

Fears that food stocks in the city would run out caused race enthusiasts to bring their own livestock. Chickens galore pecked at the Knavesmire grass before providing St Leger dinners. Hotels and cafes took in as much extra food as they were able. Brewers' ten-ton drays, fully laden, catered for the big, heavy thirst.

The great day itself presented an unending mass of faces. The crowd was estimated at between one hundred and fifty and two hundred thousand. So great was the crush that placing a bet was a work of art.

Those who strained to watch the saddling could see no more than the

The parade ring. (Alec Russell)

York at its most splendid. (Fred Spencer)

Lester Piggott and Jupiter Island win the 1983 Tote Ebor. (Gerry Cranham)

Habibti (Willie Carson) in the lead in the William Hill Sprint which they won, 1983. (Gerry Cranham)

jockey's caps. The crowd stretched down the finishing straight for more than three furlongs, and they were still pouring in. Pressure was so great that some people broke onto the course itself. Good-natured jostling became edged with desperation, and desperation developed into hysteria as part of the crowd tried to rush the turnstiles. Police fought their way through to prevent chaos.

Depression so often follows euphoria, and a large number of dejected faces turned from the finishing straight and made their way to the starting gate. They groaned on discovering that it was almost as difficult to witness the start. The rails were packed for two furlongs. Only one thing for it – peep over the shoulders of those who ringed the rest of the course.

Back in the paddock the crush was almost unimaginable as generals were squashed against corporals. At the unsaddling, people strove so much for vantage points that those who sat on the county stand railings nearly had their legs broken.

At the start of the big race a hush descended on the great crowd. It was as though something awe-inspiring, even sacred, was to manifest itself – an eclipse of the sun or the advent of some messiah.

Uniforms of all ranks stood to attention. Some were propped up with crutches, some had empty sleeves. This was not the time for fashions, as the peace was still being won.

Silence followed the horses round. There were murmurings of excitement as Rising Light, the King's horse, began his challenge. But the murmurs grew no louder as Squadron-Leader Stanhope Joel's Chamossaire came first to the post. It was as though the crowd could not grasp the reality of what was before them. They'd seen something similar at the cinema, or read about it in some sporting magazine.

Dick Perryman, who had ridden a fine pre-war race at York, was Chamossaire's trainer. As Tommy Lowrey, the winning jockey, dismounted in the unsaddling enclosure, the ring of hands clapped politely, as if over-exuberance would be a sign of disrespect.

Squadron-Leader Stanhope Joel's Chamossaire (T. Lowrey up) wins the St Leger.

The Gimcrack and Ebor provided a great double for Lord Derby and for jockey Harry Wragg. Harry had a length to spare on Gulf Stream in the Gimcrack, and sailed home on Wayside Inn in the Ebor.

When the last race was over and the huge crowd had melted away by train, bus and the occasional motor car, Knavesmire was a scene of torn-up race-cards and empty food-bags.

Half a million people had crammed into York for that three-day meeting – the curtain-raiser on post-war racing. 'St Leger week in York,' observed the *Yorkshire Gazette*, 'was a tonic for thousands. And, for the squeamish we did make one sacrifice – we did not illuminate the ancient walls.'

Whether one could view Manny Shinwell's directive as being squeamish is debatable. But directive it was, and York Corporation had certainly offered no sacrifice.

Knavesmire, however, had met the challenge. Now for the challenges to come.

A period of 'wait and see' followed. A Race Committee, which had more than survived the traumas of the war years, was content to lick its wounds for a while.

In 1946 Harry Wragg followed up his Gimcrack success on board Petition, which was carrying the identical weight to the previous year's winner. In the same year, Lord Irwin, later to become Lord Halifax, shook off the war to become a member of York Race Committee.

The problem with which York was still faced was so old as to be part of its character. The land on which the races were held was owned by York Corporation. The course was even, testing the demands of a sensitive spirit-level, a dream world for those who expected the best in flat racing.

Everyone knew its quality, but what confidence in investment could there be while an ever watchful Corporation studied the direction of the wind, refusing to grant a lease of meaningful significance?

The arrival of the fifties left this problem unsolved. The decade made its debut with what became known, somewhat begrudgingly, as the 'year of the French'. This was reflected in the Gimcrack Stakes, the sequel to which was the Gimcrack Dinner speech by the winning owner, Monsieur Marcel Boussac, whose Cortil had carried off the August prize.

It was not long before a distinctly English flavour was added to the proceedings. And what could be more appropriate than the 'royal touch'?

Only a few months after gaining accession to the throne, in 1952, Queen Elizabeth II, had her first winner at York. Harry Carr, riding Aureole to victory in the Acomb Stakes, established a prolonged association between the Queen and York racecourse.

In the meantime a now extremely mature Gordon Richards obliged by winning the Glasgow Stakes for the Queen on Rejoicing, two years after the Coronation. Glasgow the Volcano was not there to witness the event.

In that year of 1954 Knavesmire had good reason to recall the heavy

An all-too frequent scene in the winter, when the course is often flooded.

conditions with which it had been associated in the distant past. The August meeting was hit by what those who were brave enough to be present described as a monsoon.

Wally Swinburn had the task of piloting By Thunder! (the name itself must have been indicative to the intuitive) in the Ebor Handicap. Wally coped with a virtually flooded course, bringing home his mount to thunderous applause.

The following year the Queen was back among the winners. This time her colours were carried by an earnest, dedicated young fellow called Lester Piggott, who won the Askham Sweeps on Annie Oakley.

Piggott's affection for Knavesmire, which would become his favourite course, roughly coincided with the Queen's fascination for York. A wide, galloping course, affording no advantage in the draw, it was to bring out the best from Piggott in many a race.

This tall, shrewd connoisseur of horse-flesh, who could often be seen in York sampling a cigar and coffee for his main course, was to exploit a barely perceptible characteristic of Knavesmire – the slight bend a few yards from home.

159

More than one race he would win by switching to the left in the final strides to grab those coveted few inches.

Piggott was faintly reminiscent of the even taller 'Tin Man', Fred Archer, who had won the Gimcrack three times back in the late 19th century.

Knavesmire also proved a happy hunting-ground for Irish trainer Paddy Prendergast, who won the Gimcrack in 1951 and 1953 with Windy City and The Pie King respectively. His successes in England were resented. After an inquiry into one of his horses, Black Sail, the Jockey Club ruled that any horse trained by him would not be allowed to race under rules.

The Irish Turf Club, not surprisingly, backed Prendergast, and the Jockey Club altered its decision. When Prendergast's ban was lifted, in August 1954, he celebrated by sending ten horses over to the York meeting. Four of them won!

Everything was jogging along at a reasonably happy pace, but York Race Committee's dream of escaping from the straight-jacket of a short-term lease still seemed unlikely to be realised.

When Lord Irwin, who perpetually dwelt on those golden days of Lord Rockingham and the gallant Gimcrack, succeeded Lord Zetland as chairman of the Race Committee in the mid-fifties, he realised what faced him – a lease which was to expire in 1963, and York Corporation, most of whose representatives were longing to get their hands on the course.

Now was the moment, the precise moment, for the new combination which was to transform York. Major Leslie Petch retired as senior judge to the Jockey Club to become Clerk of the Course at York.

The man who, as a novice flyer, had performed that impetuous loop-the-loop, was given a free hand, by Lord Irwin and the committee, to use his enterprise for the benefit of Knavesmire.

Everyone realised that the pace of improvements needed had to be quickened to a gallop, and who better to force the pace than the 'Galloping Major' himself?

The uniqueness of York lay, and still lies, in its ability to combine the predictable with the unpredictable – to innovate events and yet retain the charm of the old ones.

Petch was quick to detect the restless atmosphere at Knavesmire: he and the committee were, indeed, both an expression and a cause of it. 'York', he announced, 'is York, with a great past and, I hope, an even greater future.'

But the key to the door of radical change lay in the granting of a long lease, and Leslie Petch, who was to travel the world on behalf of York races, was fully aware of this.

In the autumn of 1956 York City Council was faced with a now familiar debate. The Race Committee wished to take a firm step forward, but was confronted by the merry-go-round obstacle of the lease's expiry – this time due in 1963.

Every such approach to the council was fraught with danger, serving to rekindle the old discussion of a Corporation takeover. But any application

The visit of H.M. Queen Elizabeth The Queen Mother and H.R.H. The Princess Royal, 17 May 1961. With Queen Elizabeth is Lord Halifax and accompanying the Princess Royal is Capt. Sir Cecil Boyd-Rochfort the royal trainer.

for a renewed lease had to be made well in advance. The remaining seven years of guaranteed life were insufficient to justify investment in anything bigger than a flea circus.

The Race Committee put in for the familiar thirty-year stretch – not too little, and not so great as to cause alarm among those of the council who had fairly moderate views on the subject. The majority of the council seemed to be itching for control, but their Parks Committee – the group who had day-to-day dealings with the racecourse – advised that the Race Committee should be given the lease.

Twice the application was shelved. Never had Knavesmire's future been more in the balance. Eventually the corporation conceded. But it was the end of another skirmish, not of the battle. Thirty years was the lease requested and that was exactly what the Race Committee was to get. Everyone would go through the whole routine again in the eighties.

Well, it formed a breathing space, enabling certain improvements to be made. But there was hardly justification for sweeping, massive improvements. The racecourse was still on the hook.

In the meantime, the racing was maintaining its quality. Lord Zetland's retirement as Race Committee chairman caused many to recall his rather impetuous ancestor, the owner of Voltigeur.

The Great Voltigeur Stakes for colts, styled 'Great' in the same year that the new lease was granted, were becoming almost as evocative as the Gimcrack Stakes. They were also being won by some great horses, seven of which, during the late fifties and early sixties, went on to win the St Leger.

The Yorkshire Oaks, a splendid one-and-a-half mile race for three-year-old fillies, featured at the same August meeting as the Voltigeur, but had many more whiskers. It had started sprouting them during the 'renaissance' years of its inception – back in 1849.

The Queen completed an Oaks double in the August of 1957 when Harry Wragg steered Almeria home for her on Knavesmire, Lester Piggott having won the Epsom equivalent on Carrozza.

The great puller, the Ebor, was now being sponsored, and Lester Piggott added the 1958 event to his triumphs on the Vincent O'Brien-trained Gladness, which gave the bookies a caning, after being backed down from 10–1 to 5–1.

The Great Voltigeur of that year witnessed the power of Alcido, withdrawn from the Derby for which it was strongly fancied. Alcido put in a tremendous performance, romping home by twelve lengths.

Back came Piggott with the royal touch the following year, when the Queen's Pindari took the Voltigeur. Meanwhile, as the fifties were fading out, a new stand yawned out towards the course, spear-heading a variety of improvements, catering both for creature comforts and for the racing.

But Petch, who couldn't stand still for more than about two seconds, and who had a never-ending stream of ideas, was faced by that sickening restriction of the limited lease.

The rural scene at Garrowby Hall, near York, family seat of the Halifax family, had a nostalgic appeal, evoking those precious occasions in Victorian days when squire and tenant lifted glasses together to baptise some happy occurrence.

It was a pleasant autumnal day in 1959. Under a huge marquee, high teas of ham and roast turkey were sprawled along endless rows of tables. The grounds were thronged with hundreds of guests, tenants and estate workers.

Gold tulips and laburnum had been planted to mark the golden wedding anniversary of Lord and Lady Halifax. The Earl, already a sick man, had suffered an additional, ominous handicap by breaking his thigh in a fall while gardening.

He watched the proceedings from a wheelchair, and as the evening sun dipped away he reflected on his hunting days with his eldest son Charles, Lord Irwin, who had an added passion for horse racing.

Lord Halifax, home where he belonged, recalled those troubled wartime days when he was British Ambassador in America. 'Here, in Yorkshire,' he had observed, during an interlude at Garrowby, 'is a true fragment of the undying England. Is it possible that the Prussian jackboot will force its way into this countryside to tread and trample over it at will?'

The evening sun had dipped away, and the fireworks fizzled, crackled and shot. He remembered the mesmeric madman at Berchtesgarten, in whom he had striven to catch some sign of integrity.

His mind strayed further – to India, and to a man full of integrity called Gandhi. As Viceroy, the then Lord Irwin had failed to communicate with the mystical leader who advocated non-co-operation as a means to his country's independence.

The aloof English aristocrat versus the captivating idealist. Had he been too aloof? Possibly, but it had been his duty as Viceroy to have Gandhi arrested after that symbolic, defiant, illegal gesture of making salt.

Lord Halifax recalled how he had assessed Gandhi: 'There was a directness about him which was singularly winning, but this could be accompanied by a subtlety of intellectual process which could be sometimes disconcerting.'

But now Lord Halifax, former Viceroy of India, Foreign Secretary and Ambassador to the United States, was back at Garrowby. And his mind

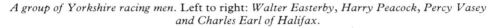

A group of Yorkshire racing men. Left to right: *Walter Easterby, Harry Peacock, Percy Vasey and Charles Earl of Halifax.*

turned to its ultimate resting place – the soft Yorkshire Wolds, the hunting, the farming and this delightful garden party.

Three months later Lord Halifax died, the title passing to his eldest son Charles, chairman of York Race Committee. The late Lord Halifax had been the statesman with a fondness for English rural life.

The new Lord Halifax, epitome of Englishmen's conception of a gentle, country squire, devoted much of his enthusiasm and energy to Knavesmire.

The Halifax-Petch campaign was on. Lord Halifax did the guiding, Major Petch the hunting. The first obstacle to clear was the limited lease. Sweeping improvements were planned, and in 1962 back went the Race Committee to the meeting chamber.

The negotiations were tough and prolonged but, at long last, a piece of eternity was achieved, in the shape of a lease which would not run out until January 1, in the year 2056!

20

Security... at last

In day in May, 1965 came a day which York races had been awaiting for centuries. The greatest development in the history of the racecourse had been completed, and was very much in evidence – a huge, six-tier grandstand.

The graft had started immediately after the last race the previous August. One day the crowds were milling around to watch the finishes, scurrying to place last-minute bets. The next day, in moved the demolition men to pound the way clear for the new giant and its ancillaries.

As the winter began to melt away, the stand of the future began to raise its head – a Wembley stadium of racing with the Grand Hotel touch.

York had sprinted towards the long straight ahead, and those present at the opening ceremony who cared to glance to where the Knavesmire course turned into the home straight could see another innovation – a seven-furlong course which jutted out towards the village of Bishopthorpe.

'It's been a close-run thing,' Lord Halifax announced to a beaming audience, 'but York's stand is here for all to see. I can't help feeling sad that part of the old facade of the York stands is no more. York has always had a unique atmosphere, blending the old-fashioned with the modern (part of John Carr's old stand stood politely by), and we'll endeavour to preserve this atmosphere.'

There was triumph in the air as the chairman of the Turf Board, Major-General Sir Randle Feilden, described the occasion, in best military style, as York's finest hour.

The opening of this ultra-modern building had been performed by Lord Halifax, member of a family whose involvement in racing at York went back to the days when there was no grandstand at all, to those days when early-eighteenth century floods caused havoc on the ings.

Curtain up on the new era: the following afternoon crowds flocked to surroundings both familiar and new to witness the start of the first race – the Dante Stakes.

'The entries are colossal', announced Leslie Petch before the opening of that year's October meeting. The man who could be seen busying himself around Longchamp and Santa Anita in an effort to pick up new ideas, was never content to stand, or sit still.

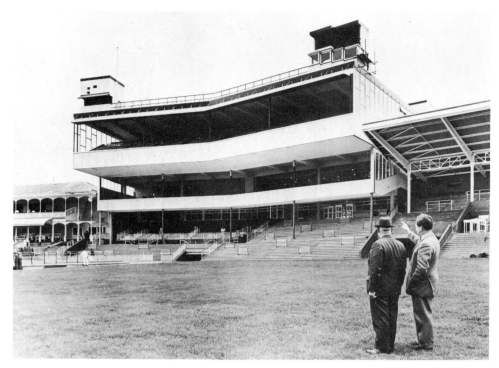

Major Leslie Petch and Tim Thompson (right), *Racing Information Bureau P.R.O. for the North, admiring the new stand.*

More improvements were planned. But on one point York stood firm – there would be no racing round the calendar, for which so many were eager. The emphasis was on quality flat racing – the best flat racing. And winter flooding, combined with racing, would be detrimental to that aim.

By the following year, 1966, the sponsor-chaser needed an assistant manager, a job which fell to the Galloping Major's nephew, John Sanderson, a Lincolnshire-born chartered accountant with a deep love of racing, who was to become the youngest clerk of the course in the country.

Sanderson, who started to watch racing as a child, was quite unlike Leslie Petch. For, whereas Petch could not stand still for two seconds, Sanderson couldn't sit still for a second. Leslie Petch was the mentor, and John Sanderson the pupil. And the baton was ready to be handed over when the need arose.

While the sporting connoisseur found the racing at York increasingly to his taste, the gourmet's palate was being placated too. The county-stand catering was beginning to echo the Rockingham era. At one August meeting in the sixties huge amounts of beef, pork and lamb were trundled in, together

Major Petch (right) *with John Sanderson.*

with four hundred grouse, three hundred and fifty chickens, one hundred Norfolk ducklings, five hundred pounds of Scotch salmon, five hundred dover sole, four hundred lobster and one hundred and fifty pounds of smoked salmon.

Meanwhile, back on the course, the Queen was managing to bag her share of winners, including the Yorkshire Cup and the Fitzwilliam Stakes. Fitzwilliam: a name which smacked of boisterous days, and of gloomy ones. The Lord Fitzwilliam of 1796, inheritor of the Rockingham estates, joined in that night of near debauchery at York Tavern, when liquor of every hue soaked every brain into a common pool of stupor.

The Fitzwilliams had sought their pleasure elsewhere when Knavesmire snored through the 1830s. 'We regret to observe', stated *The New Sporting Magazine* of those sad times, 'that the Fitzwilliam, Harewood, and other noble families, going with the stream, have withdrawn their countenance from a meeting which ought to be the rallying point for all who regard the interests of the county.

'It will suffice to say that the August meeting turned out to be a miserable

On 28 June 1971 H.M. The Queen drove down the course when she attended the celebrations for the 1900th anniversary of the founding of the City of York.

failure, the company consisting of one Lord, one baronet, four or five captains and about a dozen private gentlemen.'

The Queen celebrated the dawn of the seventies at York by winning the Eglinton Stakes with the combination of Charlton and Joe Mercer. Eglinton: a name which recalled that gargantuan clash between Lord Eglinton's Flying Dutchman and Lord Zetland's Voltigeur.

The same year of 1970 welcomed the great Mill Reef to York, when it became one of the most successful winners in the history of the Gimcrack Stakes, going on to win both the Derby and the Prix de l'Arc de Triomphe.

Mill Reef interrupted a run of successes in this prestigious event by millionaire owner David Robinson, who gained pride of place at the Gimcrack Dinner in 1968, 1969 and 1971 with Tudor Music, Yellow God and Wishing Star respectively.

The Gimcrack Club, the oldest Turfing fraternity of all, comprising hunting enthusiasts, racing devotees and bons viveurs, who had in common a liking for that little grey horse in the sky, had first met to dine back in 1770.

Their descendants, exactly two hundred years later, leaned contentedly back to hear their chief guest, Charles, Prince of Wales, state that if he ever

RACING RECORD OF MILL REEF

AT 2: WON SALISBURY, COVENTRY, GIMCRACK, IMPERIAL AND
DEWHURST STAKES, SECOND IN PRIX ROBERT PAPIN.
AT 3: WON GREENHAM, DERBY, ECLIPSE, KING GEORGE VI AND
QUEEN ELIZABETH STAKES AND PRIX DE L'ARC DE TRIOMPHE
SECOND TO BRIGADIER GERARD IN TWO THOUSAND GUINEAS
AT 4: WON PRIX GANAY AND CORONATION CUP.

John Skeaping's statue of Mill Reef which is in the Racing Museum, York.

raced horses, as his namesake Charles II had done, it would definitely be on the flat. 'I'm terrified of jumping horses.'

President of the Gimcrack Club, Lord Halifax, found himself in a sticky spot the following year when what might have been a broad hint was taken as such by David Robinson, that year's winning owner.

Mr Robinson took the huff at the implication that he should cut his speech to five minutes. He refused to attend – a refusal almost akin to declining a request to pay his taxes.

A second letter hastily followed. Mr Robinson would of course be welcome 'even if you speak for only five minutes.' The difference between asking him to make it snappy and suggesting that he should was a subtle one – sufficient enough, however, to enable Mr Robinson to change his mind with dignity. A modern crisis had been averted.

In the same year, that great driving force behind York's progress, Major Leslie Petch, suffered a sudden illness and retired as clerk of course.

At twenty-nine years of age John Sanderson, a former point-to-point rider, who had become involved in racing administration by helping out at York and other northern courses on race days, took over the role.

Meanwhile the ground had been laid for a new race which was to prove

H.R.H. The Prince of Wales with the Lord Mayor of York at the Gimcrack Dinner 1970.

the cherry on top of the icing. York gained the sponsorship of cigarette and tobacco manufacturers, Benson and Hedges, for a top-class event over one mile, two-and-a-half furlongs. The world's best three-year-old colts and fillies were eligible.

The Benson and Hedges Gold Cup was to be the ace of the racing season – one which was to be both the supreme test for the finest horses and a source of constant surprise. It would provoke discussion – sometimes heated, sometimes reflective. But it would never be boring.

The first running of the Benson and Hedges Gold Cup attracted the attention of the entire racing world, bringing together Roberto and the 'unbeatable' Brigadier Gerard.

It was a meeting which Knavesmire had been awaiting for nearly two hundred and fifty years. And the temptation to attend the full three days of the meeting proved too great for Queen Elizabeth II. York races had arrived.

21

Knavesmire-An Exciting Future

 His narration finished, the man led his two sons down the long-distance straight towards the two-mile marker, the towers of York Minster ahead peering over the avenue of trees. They were among the stragglers of that day's huge racing crowd.

The boys were silent as they reflected on what their father had said.

'Well', said one of them eventually, 'if that's the end then nobody needs to worry any more.'

'I didn't say that it was the end of the story,' said the father. 'I said that

---

York Race Committee, 1983. Left to right: *R. A. Bethell, S. E. Scrope, Lord Manton, M. W. Wickham-Boynton (chairman), the Marquis of Zetland, L. B. Holliday, the Earl of Halifax.*

172

John Sanderson, Secretary/Manager and Clerk of the Course.

York races had arrived. That's a different matter. If they start getting smug and crow about being better than all the other racecourses put together, then they'll fall into the trap that they fell into all those years ago'.

'You mean they'd start hanging people again?' asked the other son.

'No', laughed the father, 'they've stopped all that now. What I mean is that they would get soft – like a man who is so happy about becoming slim that he eats all the things that had made him fat in the first place.'

'It's not the end then?'

'No, it's a new beginning. But, really, there's no beginning and no end. Just life. And racing should be about life. Anyway, would you like to start going racing?'

The boys said they would and the Benson and Hedges Gold Cup of 1972 proved their initiation ceremony at Knavesmire. They were peeping over the rails in much the same way as the new Clerk of Course, John Sanderson, had done back in his own childhood days at Lincoln.

Unshackled and uninhibited, York broke into a loose gallop, then a broad gallop, then a full-bellied sprint. The thunder of Knavesmire hooves was heard across Britain, then Europe, then the world. Even the Polish were here, to the delight of the Race Committee and to the dismay of the race commentator.

The Gold Cup added sparks of lightning to the thunder. In 1972 French premier jockey Yves St Martin came to ride Rheingold. Lester Piggott had been Vincent O'Brien's choice to partner Roberto, but soft ground, said O'Brien, ruled Roberto out.

Piggott ultimately accepted the Rheingold ride, having agreed to partner Moulton. There was sympathy for St Martin, and it was ironic that Moulton, with Geoff Lewis up, should take the prize, with Rheingold, back in third place, four lengths behind. But Lester and Rheingold gained considerable consolation through winning the subsequent Arc de Triomphe.

The Earl of Halifax's Shirley Heights (Greville Starkey up) wins the 1978 Mecca-Dante Stakes.

Hawaiian Sound after winning the Benson and Hedges Gold Cup, 1978.

Lester had good reason to favour York. He took the Benson and Hedges Gold Cup in the two following years – a remarkable double since he was on board an equally remarkable filly, Dahlia.

Back bounced Piggott in 1978 to win the Benson and Hedges Gold Cup on Hawaiian Sound. But the sound which welcomed this victory served to echo the triumphs, that very year, of probably the most celebrated three-year-old in racing – Shirley Heights.

Only two years before his death, gentle Lord Halifax, chairman of York Race Committee, experienced the delight of a fading lifetime when Shirley Heights carried his colours first past the post in the Derby.

This superb stallion, bred at the Garrowby Stud near York, gave English bloodstock and Yorkshire racing a tremendous boost by becoming the fifth horse in racing history to win both the England and Irish Derby. And there had been no greater excitement on Knavesmire than when Shirley Heights, with Greville Starkey up, won the Mecca-Dante Stakes, York's Derby trial.

Hawaiian Sound had a good chance to look at Shirley Heights, losing by a head to him in the Derby and by a head and a neck in the Irish Derby.

That effusive, larger-than-his-suit New Yorker, Leone J Peters, was about to abandon English racing when he sampled the delights of Knavesmire and the glory of being half-owner of the Benson and Hedges Gold Cup winner.

His polka-dot tie beaming in the sunshine, Leone J Peters boomed, 'There's no European track to compare with York, and the great facilities provided here don't exist on American tracks. It was York, and not my interest in Hawaiian Sound, that won me over to your English racing.'

Leone J, who had just witnessed Piggott's triumph, then risked the resurrection of the Tyburn by exclaiming, 'Willie Shoemaker is the greatest jockey in the world.'

Meanwhile, the Queen was dropping in with increasing regularity, appreciating, no doubt, a welcome which was warm without being over-bearing. Her twenty-fifth York victory came, however, just after her Silver Jubilee year.

There were golden celebrations too. Joe Limb, an ex-miner, and his wife Doris were given a special treat to mark their fifty years of marriage. They were driven from their home in Derbyshire to lunch in the county stand before watching the racing from a private box.

The most humbly-dressed on Knavesmire could always be given finer clothes, and the promotion of a race, which had started in 1908 as a modest selling plate, to the richest sprint event in Europe, proved a star example of York's enterprise.

The Nunthorpe Stakes became, in 1976, the five-furlong William Hill Sprint Championship, with that popular Yorkshire jockey Eddie Hide partnering the first two winners of the event – Lochnager and Haveroid. Lochnager, and the 1978 winner Solinus, partnered by Piggott, were the top sprinters of their respective years.

Knavesmire never lost its touch of poignancy. Bill Grainger, who had spent the last fifteen years of his life, working for the Earl of Halifax out at Garrowby Hall, had his last wish granted when his ashes were scattered round the winning post. A bouquet, at the base of the post, which bore testimony to his death-wish, rustled imperceptibly as hooves thundered past it throughout the Ebor meeting of 1976.

Four years later, the gentle squire himself died at the age of sixty-seven after returning from a holiday in the West Indies.

Charles Ingram Courtenay Wood had never aspired to be other than what he felt he should be – sociable landowner, supporter of country sports and of the Turf and champion of the established church. To some these aims might seem unimaginative, but at least they form a principle, in a world where many adapt their principles to suit the convenience of the moment.

He was High Steward of York Minister, the setting for a memorial service which recalled the final tributes to earlier figures who had made their mark on York's racing scene. Rockingham, Melrose, Halifax – the Minister towers ultimately welcomed them all.

As you look out from the shoulders of the chalky Yorkshire Wolds, these same towers beckon in the near distance. But beneath you, snuggled between grassy hillocks sleeps the trim, tiny church of Kirby Underdale. And it was in the peaceful garden of this church, on the Garrowby estate, that Lord Halifax was buried, while the tree-lined stream murmured through the past into the future.

Past, present, future – all formed a timeless pattern as Knavesmire galloped on and on.

Sharpo, with Pat Eddery up, brought the crowd to its feet in 1981, beating such daunting opposition as Morestyle and Marwell, to complete a double in that exhilarating Sprint Championship. A year to remember at York for Eddery, who also drove home the Gold Cup winner Beldale Flutter.

A year full of double delights, as Lester Piggott continued to entertain on his favourite course, steering home the great Ardross to the first Yorkshire Cup double in the fifty years of the race's history.

York could always pause to pay tributes. Racing on Knavesmire was now two hundred and fifty years old. This was a time for self-congratulations and for a little acknowledgement, in the form of a special race named after High Line, four of whose progeny – Master Willie, Shoot a Line, Cocaine and Heighlin – had all won races on the opening day of the previous year's August meeting.

That old favourite, the Ebor, continued to satisfy popular sympathy, and that equally popular grand all-rounder, Sea Pigeon, couldn't end his career without landing the big one at Knavesmire. His perpetual partner, Jonjo O'Neill, partnered him to victory in 1979.

But that celebration year of 1981 was the most eventful in recent times. As York's August meeting opened, the Queen's jockey, chirpy Willie Carson, looked set to take the jockey's crown again, being appreciably ahead of Lester Piggott, his nearest rival.

When the cherubic-faced Carson entered the final straight on Silken Knot in the Yorkshire Oaks he little realised how close to oblivion he was.

Silken Knot crashed to the floor as one leg cracked. Another leg broke as high velocity was brought to an abrupt, sickening halt. Carson was catapulted into the path of a thundering group. Five horses trampled the little silk-clad bundle.

Ambulancemen, vets, officials, rushed towards the inert body as the field raced on towards the grandstand. Silken Knot, floundering helplessly had to be destroyed. Carson had a fracture at the bottom of his skull. Other parts of the spinal column had been broken, as well as his left wrist.

Sea Pigeon (no 1) goes to post before the 1979 Tote Ebor.

The crowd waited anxiously for some unofficial bulletin on one of the most popular jockeys in racing history. A great cheer lifted the meeting back to jollity as it was announced that Carson had regained consciousness and was out of danger.

Willie had escaped death by a fraction – one so small as to be immeasurable. But the main thing that galled him as he lay in hospital was how he'd let that title slip into Piggott's hands.

Back he came the following year – the year in which Pope John Paul the Second made a helicopter landing on Knavesmire before addressing a mass audience there.

York had its own jockeys' championship, and Willie was determined to pip the main contenders – Lester Piggott and an immensely successful American youngster called Steve Cauthen, who had also decided that York was his favourite English racecourse.

A certain grand old man of York racing would have rejoiced to see Carson win the Melrose Stakes during his fight back. The name of the winning horse, Broken Rail, gave pause for reflection. Willie needed to make up a lot

Lester Piggott (left) and Willie Carson, both of whom have ridden many winners at York.

of ground at the August meeting – the one which had seen him close to death the previous year. Carson scorned previous ill luck with a vengeance, bringing home four winners, including the Queen's Sans Blague in the Galtres Stakes. Two months later that York title was his.

Knavesmire went into its winter sleep, and during those short, early days of 1983 that other partner in York's revival went to his rest.

Major Leslie Petch, the bustling, hard-of-hearing entrepreneur, who had teamed up with the gentle squire to put Knavesmire back on its feet, was buried near his home at Loftus in north-east Yorkshire.

Ill health had snatched him from full-blooded administration, but as a member of the Race Committee, Petch the farmer was able to witness the harvest that he had helped to reap. Thousands, millions more were to reap the benefit too. And those who reaped would, in their turn, help to sow.

Among them were two young men who, as boys, had been told the Knavesmire story more than a decade previously.

It was a warm, languid day, only a few months after the death of Leslie

During his tour of Britain in 1982 Pope Paul II attended an open air mass on Knavesmire.

Petch. The air was charged with racing, and the two were wandering along the rails towards the starting stalls. A group of small boys watched open-mouthed as a stream of equine muscle rippled past them, topped by multi-coloured blobs of living ice-cream.

One of the lads turned his mouth from the rails. 'Hey, mister,' he called to one of the men. 'Somebody was bragging to us about this being the best racecourse in the country. Is that right?'

'Yes lad,' was the reply.

'Why's that?'

There was a pause.

'Well, probably because it nearly wasn't.'

'What do you mean.'

The two men smiled, and looked towards each other. 'Bang goes the afternoon', said one. 'But it's the least we can do.'

So they brought the boys over, sat down, looked back towards the Tyburn marker and started to tell them a story. It went something like this . . .

The following photographs help to capture the personalities that give Knavesmire its character.

R. Atkinson, telephon-
ist from starting gate
to weighing room.

Major M. Eveleigh,
starter.

Teddy-bear stand out-side the course.

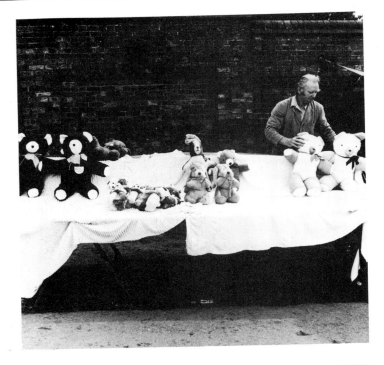

Temporary gatemen waiting to receive their badges and instruc-tions.

Bookmaker.

Painters working on the course before the start of the season.

Appendix-Principal Winners

DANTE STAKES 1958–1975
MECCA–DANTE STAKES 1976–1983

1958 H F Guggenheim's Bald
    Eagle (W H Carr)

1959 Lady Zia Wernher's Dickens
    (W H Carr)

1960 Sir V Sassoon's St Paddy
    (L Piggott)

1961 H J Joel's Gallant Knight
    (E Smith)

1962 W H Cockerline's Lucky
    Brief (B Connorton)

1963 Sir F Robinson's Merchant
    Venturer (G Starkey)

1964 Lady Sassoon's Sweet Moss
    (L Piggott)

1965 W T Stoker's Ballymarais
    (W Pyers)

1966 R D Hollingsworth's
    Hermes (G Starkey)

1967 A B Askew's Gay Garland
    (R Hutchinson)

1968 C B Nathhorst's Lucky
    Finish (B Taylor)

1969 Duke of Sutherland's
    Activator (M Thomas)

1970 Sir H de Trafford's
    Approval (G Starkey)

1971 J Dellal's Fair World
    (J Lindley)

1972 H R K Zeisel's Rheingold
    (E Johnson)

1973 L Freedman's Owen Dudley
    (G Lewis)

1974 H J Joel's Honoured Guest
    (G Lewis)

1975 R B Moller's Hobnob
    (W Carson)

1976 J W Hickman's Trasi's Son
    (E Hide)

1977 R B & E B Moller's Lucky
    Sovereign (M L Thomas)

1978 Lord Halifax's Shirley
    Heights (G Starkey)

1979 C d'Alessio's Lyphard's
    Wish (J Mercer)

1980 D Wildenstein's Hello
    Gorgeous (J Mercer)

1981 A J Kelly's Beldale Flutter
    (P Eddery)

1982 D Wildenstein's Simply
    Great (L Piggott)

1983 E Moller's Hot Touch
    (P Eddery)

YORKSHIRE CUP 1950–1983

1950 Major H. Halmshaw's Miraculous Atom (W Nevett)
1951 T B Watson's Orderly Ann (A Carson)
1952 Lord Milford's Eastern Emperor (W Rickaby)
1953 T H Farr's Childe Harold (J Brace)
1954 Brig W P Wyatt's Premonition (W H Carr)
1955 J S Gerber's By Thunder! (W Swinburn)
1956 G W Chesterman's Romany Air (W Rickaby)
1957 R F Dennis's Souverlone (J Sime)
1958 W Humble's Brioche (E Britt)
1959 R D Hollingsworth's Cutter (E Mercer)
1960 Lady Zia Wernher's Dickens (W H Carr)
1961 H Warwick Daw's Pandofell (L Piggott)
1962 Lady G Cholmondeley's Sagacity (W H Carr)
1963 Mrs E C Gaze's Honour Bound (D Smith)
1964 P A B Widener's Raise You Ten (W H Carr)
1965 H M The Queen's Apprentice (S Clayton)
1966 Lt Col J Hornung's Aunt Edith (L Piggott)

1967 G A Oldham's Salvo (R Hutchinson)
1968 Duke of Roxburghe's Sweet Story (J Etherington)
1969 H L Vickery's Quartette (R Maddock)
1970 Lady Sassoon's Rangong (A Barclay)
1971 V Barclay's Alto Volante (B Taylor)
1972 Major V McCalmont's Knockroe (L Piggott)
1973 Mrs S Hick's Celtic Cone (G Starkey)
1974 R D Hollingworth's Buoy (J Mercer)
1975 Lady Beaverbrook's Riboson (J Mercer)
1976 C A B St George's Bruni (L Piggott)
1977 J H Whitney's Bright Finish (L Piggott)
1978 Lord Porchester's Smuggler (W Carson)
1979 J W Rowles's Pragmatic (J Reid)
1980 R R Guest's Noble Saint (L Piggott)
1981 C A B St George's Ardross (L Piggott)
1982 C A B St George's Ardross (L Piggott)
1983 N Hetherton's Line Slinger (E Hide)

JOHN SMITH'S MAGNET CUP 1960–1983

1960 R Booth's Fougalle (N McIntosh)
1961 Major L B Holliday's Proud Chieftain (W H Carr)
1962 Major L B Holliday's Nortia (F Durr)

1963 L G Lazarus's Raccolto (J Sime)
1964 J Crow's Space King (E Hide)
1965 M Sobell's Dark Court (A Breasley)

1966 J Fisher's David Jack
   (P Robinson)
1967 H F Hartley's Copsale
   (L G Brown)
1968 W G Barker's Farm Walk
   (J Seagrave)
1969 A G M Stevens's My Swanee
   (L Piggott)
1970 Lord Rosebery's Timon
   (G Welsh)
1971 Col P L M Wright's
   Prominent (G Baxter)
1972 Col P L M Wright's
   Prominent (G Baxter)
1973 Col W E Behrens's Peleid
   (M L Thomas)
1974 A Villar's Take a Reef
   (G Baxter)

1975 Mrs J Bricken's Jolly Good
   (W Carson)
1976 Sir M Sobell's Bold Pirate
   (J Mercer)
1977 S Wingfield Digby's Air
   Trooper (M L Thomas)
1978 Lord Porchester's Town &
   Country (W Carson)
1979 Mrs P L Yong's Tesoro Mio
   (E Hide)
1980 W Hobson's Fine Sun
   (N Howe)
1981 G L Cambanis's Amyndas
   (T Lucas)
1982 Mrs V M McKinney's
   Buzzard's Bay (M Birch)
1983 Lord Halifax's Bedtime
   (W Carson)

BENSON AND HEDGES GOLD CUP 1972–1983

1972 J W Galbreath's Roberto
   (B Baeza)
1973 R Moller's Moulton
   (G Lewis)
1974 N B Hunt's Dahlia
   (L Piggott)
1975 N B Hunt's Dahlia
   (L Piggott)
1976 C d'Alessio's Wollow
   (G Dettori)
1977 Lady Beaverbrook's Relkino
   (W Carson)

1978 R Sangster's Hawaiian
   Sound (L Piggott)
1979 Sir M Sobell's Troy
   (W Carson)
1980 W Barnett's Master Willie
   (P Waldron)
1981 A Kelly's Beldale Flutter
   (P Eddery)
1982 R Sangster's Assert
   (P Eddery)
1983 R Sangster's Caerleon
   (P Eddery)

YORKSHIRE OAKS 1950–1983

1950 H M The King's Above
   Board (E Smith)
1951 Lt Col G Loder's Sea Parrot
   (G Richards)
1952 Capt A Keith's Frieze
   (E Britt)
1953 H H Aga Khan's Kerkeb
   (G Richards)

1954 J McGrath's Feevagh
   (K Gethin)
1955 R Hollingworth's Ark Royal
   (E Mercer)
1956 J Astor's Indian Twilight
   (J Mercer)
1957 H M The Queen's Almeria
   (W H Carr)

1958 Maj L B Holiday's None
Nicer (S Clayton)
1959 Prince Aly Khan's Petite
Etoile (L Piggott)
1960 Mrs E Fawcett's Lynchris
(W Williamson)
1961 Mrs W Riley-Smith's
Tenacity (A Breasley)
1962 H J Joel's West Side Story
(E Smith)
1963 Major J Priestman's
Outcrop (E Smith)
1964 Sir F Robinson's Homeward
Bound (G Starkey)
1965 G Williams's Mabel
(J Mercer)
1966 Mrs W Riley-Smith's
Parthian Glance
(L Piggott)
1967 Dr C Vittadini's Palatch
(B Taylor)
1968 Mrs R Midwood's Exchange
(B Taylor)
1969 C Spence's Frontier
Goddess (D Keith)
1970 Mrs S Joel's Lupe
(A Barclay)

1971 R Ohrstrom's Fleet Wahine
(G Lewis)
1972 L Freedman's Attica Meli
(G Lewis)
1973 G Pope Jr's Mysterious
(G Lewis)
1974 N Robinson's Dibidale
(W Carson)
1975 G Williams's May Hill
(P Eddery)
1976 Mrs J Mullion's Sarah
Siddons (C Roche)
1977 Countess M Esterhazy's
Busaca (P Eddery)
1978 S Hanson's Fair Salinia
(G Starkey)
1979 H Barker's Connaught
Bridge (J Mercer)
1980 R Budgett's Shoot a Line
(L Piggott)
1981 P Barrett's Condessa
(D Gillespie)
1982 Sheikh Mohammed Al
Maktoum's Awaasif
(L Piggott)
1983 Sir M Sobell's Sun Princess
(W Carson)

THE EBOR HANDICAP 1950–1966
JOHNNIE WALKER EBOR 1967–1973
TERRY'S ALL GOLD EBOR 1974–1975
THE TOTE EBOR HANDICAP 1976–1983

1950 Major G A Renwick's
Cadzow Oak
(J Thompson)
1951 J Hetherton's Bob (E Carter)
1952 A Bird's Signification
(H Jones)
1953 H H Aga Khan's Norooz
(R Fawdon)
1954 J Gerber's By Thunder!
(W Swinburn)
1955 Miss R Olivier's Hyperion
Kid (P Robinson)

1956 Lord Rosebery's Donald
(D Smith)
1957 J Bullock's Morecambe
(J Sime)
1958 J McShain's Gladness
(L Piggott)
1959 S Joel's Primera
(L Piggott)
1960 J Whitney's Persian Road
(G Moore)
1961 Major L Gardner's Die
Hard (L Piggott)

1962 P Bull's Sostenuto
(D Morris)
1963 Mrs A Biddle's Partholon
(J Sime)
1964 Major L B Holliday's Proper
Pride (D Smith)
1965 R Moller's Twelfth Man
(P Cook)
1966 W Ruane's Lomond
(E Eldin)
1967 G Cooper's Ovaltine
(E Johnson)
1968 Lord Allendale's Alignment
(E Johnson)
1969 Mrs N Tennant's Big Hat
(R Still)
1970 Mrs R Sturdy's Tintagel II
(L Piggott)
1971 D Robinson's Knotty Pine
(F Durr)
1972 K Dodson's Crazy Rhythm
(F Durr)

1973 Mrs P Poe's Bonne Noel
(C Roche)
1974 G Coleman's Anji
(T McKeown)
1975 G Reed's Dakota (A Barclay)
1976 Mrs S Enfield's Sir Montagu
(W Carson)
1977 W G Barker's Move Off
(J Bleasdale)
1978 Lady Beaverbrook's
Totowah (P Cook)
1979 P Muldoon's Sea Pigeon
(J J O'Neill)
1980 J McCaughey's Shaftesbury
(G Starkey)
1981 S Fradkoff's Protection
Racket (M Birch)
1982 J Norman's Another Sam
(B Rouse)
1983 S M Threadwell's Jupiter
Island (L Piggott)

THE GREAT VOLTIGEUR STAKES 1950-1983

1950 Lord Rosebery's Castle
Rock (W Rickaby)
1951 Duke of Northumberland's
Border Legend
(W Nevett)
1952 T H Farr's Childe Harold
(J Brace)
1953 Brig. W P Wyatt's
Premonition
(W H Carr)
1954 G M Bell's Blue Sail
(W Rickaby)
1955 Lady Derby's Acropolis
(D Smith)
1956 Lord Astor's Hornbeam
(J Mercer)
1957 W Humble's Brioche
(E Britt)
1958 Sir H de Trafford's Alcide
(W H Carr)

1959 H M The Queen's Pindari
(L Piggott)
1960 Sir V Sassoon's St Paddy
(L Piggott)
1961 Mrs J Allen's Just Great
(A Breasley)
1962 Major L B Holliday's
Hethersett (F Durr)
1963 J R Mullion's Ragusa
(G Bougoure)
1964 C W Engelhard's Indiana
(J Lindley)
1965 E R More O'Ferrall's
Ragazzo (L Piggott)
1966 R D Hollingsworth's
Hermes (G Starkey)
1967 L M Gelb's Great Host
(W Williamson)
1968 H J Joel's Connaught
(A Barclay)

1969 Sir H Wernher's Harmony Hall (W Williamson)
1970 D Robinson's Meadowville (L Piggott)
1971 Mrs J Rogerson's Athens Wood (L Piggott)
1972 N Cohen's Our Mirage (L Piggott)
1973 R D Hollingsworth's Buoy (J Mercer)
1974 Lady Beaverbrook's Bustino (J Mercer)
1975 Dr. C Vittadini's Patch (P Eddery)
1976 L M Gelb's Hawkberry (C Roche)

1977 J Fluor's Alleged (L Piggott)
1978 H Demetriou's Whitstead (B Taylor)
1979 R Guest's Noble Saint (L Piggott)
1980 Sir M Sobell's and Lord Weinstock's Prince Bee (L Piggott)
1981 P Mellon's Glint of Gold (J Matthias)
1982 R C Clifford-Turner's and R J McCreery's Electric (W R Swinburn)
1983 P M Brant's Seymour Hicks (W. Carson)

NUNTHORPE SWEEP STAKES 1950–1976
WILLIAM HILL SPRINT CHAMPIONSHIP 1976–1983

1950 Major R Macdonald-Buchanan's Abernant (G Richards)
1951 Mrs G Kohn's Royal Serenade (C Elliott)
1952 G M Bell's Royal Serenade (G Richards)
1953 H J Joel's High Treason (D Greening)
1954 A D Winbush's My Beau (T Carter)
1955 J S Gerber's Royal Palm (W Snaith)
1956 C R Harper's Ennis (P Tulk)
1957 Major L B Holliday's Gratitude (W Snaith)
1958 G A Gilbert's Right Boy (L Piggott)
1959 H D Wills's Right Boy (L Piggott)
1960 Mrs M L Turner's Bleep-Bleep (W H Carr)
1961 Mrs J R Mullion's Floribunda (R Hutchinson)

1962 A J MacDonald's Gay Mairi (A Breasley)
1963 Mrs R C Wilson's Matatina (L Piggott)
1964 J A Done's Althrey Don (R Maddock)
1965 C J Reavey's Polyfoto (J Wilson)
1966 R F Scully's Caterina (L Piggott)
1967 Mrs W A Richardson's Forlorn River (B Raymond)
1968 D Robinson's So Blessed (F Durr)
1969 V W Hardy's Tower Walk (L Piggott)
1970 H H Renshaw's Huntercombe (A Barclay)
1971 J H Whitney's Swing Easy (L Piggott)
1972 D Robinson's Deep Diver (W Williamson)
1973 C T Olley's Sandford Lad (A Murray)

1974 R Clifford-Turner's Blue
  Cashmere (E Hide)
1975 P A V Cooper's Bay Express
  (W Carson)
1976 C F Spence's Lochnager
  (E Hide)
1977 T Newton's Haveroid
  (E Hide)
1978 D Schwartz's Solinus
  (L Piggott)

1979 Essa Alkhalifa's Ahonoora
  (G Starkey)
1980 Miss M Sheriffe's Sharpo
  (P Eddery)
1981 Miss M Sheriffe's Sharpo
  (P Eddery)
1982 Miss M Sheriffe's Sharpo
  (S Cauthen)
1983 M A A Mutawa's Habibti
  (W Carson)

THE GIMCRACK STAKES 1950–1983

1950 M Marcel Boussac's Cortil
  (W Johnstone)
1951 R Bell's Windy City
  (G Richards)
1952 J Gerber's Bebe Grande
  (W Snaith)
1953 R Bell's Pie King
  (Sir G Richards)
1954 F Ellison's Precast
  (W Nevett)
1955 D Robinson's Idle Rocks
  (D Smith)
1956 Mrs E Foster's Eudaemon
  (E Britt)
1957 P Bull's Pheidippides
  (D Smith)
1958 W Hill's Be Careful (E Hide)
1959 Mrs J Mullion's Paddy's
  Sister (G Moore)
1960 Sir A Jarvis's Test Case
  (E Larkin)
1961 Duke of Norfolk's Sovereign
  Lord (A Breasley)
1962 D van Clief's Crocket
  (D Smith)
1963 H Loebstein's Talahasse
  (L Piggott)
1964 C Engelhard's Double Jump
  (J Lindley)
1965 Mrs P Poe's Young Emperor
  (L Piggott)
1966 Mrs D Solomon's Golden
  Horus (J Mercer)

1967 Captain M Lemos's Petingo
  (L Piggott)
1968 D Robinson's Tudor Music
  (F Durr)
1969 D Robinson's Yellow God
  (F Durr)
1970 P Mellon's Mill Reef
  (G Lewis)
1971 D Robinson's Wishing Star
  (F Durr)
1972 Mrs W Richardson's Rapid
  River (T Kelsey)
1973 C St George's Giacometti
  (A Murray)
1974 R Tikkoo's Steel Heart
  (L Piggott)
1975 K Mackey's Music Boy
  (J Seagrave)
1976 N Schibbye's Nebbiolo
  (G Curran)
1977 J Wilson's
  Tumbledownwind
  (G Lewis)
1978 D Cock's Stanford (P Eddery)
1979 P Muldoon's Sonnen Gold
  (M Birch)
1980 K Abdulla's Belbolide
  (P Eddery)
1981 M Korn's Full Extent (J Lowe)
1982 A Rachid's Horage
  (A Murray)
1983 Lord Tavistock's Precocious
  (L Piggott)

Index

Names of horses in italics

193